OECD
reviews of manpower and social policies

15

manpower policy in IRELAND

ORGANISATION FOR ECONOMIC
CO-OPERATION AND DEVELOPMENT

The Organisation for Economic Co-operation and Development (OECD) was set up under a Convention signed in Paris on 14th December, 1960, which provides that the OECD shall promote policies designed :

- *to achieve the highest sustainable economic growth and employment and a rising standard of living in Member countries, while maintaining financial stability, and thus to contribute to the development of the world economy;*
- *to contribute to sound economic expansion in Member as well as non-member countries in the process of economic development;*
- *to contribute to the expansion of world trade on a multilateral, non-discriminatory basis in accordance with international obligations.*

The Members of OECD are Australia, Austria, Belgium, Canada, Denmark, Finland, France, the Federal Republic of Germany, Greece, Iceland, Ireland, Italy, Japan, Luxembourg, the Netherlands, New Zealand, Norway, Portugal, Spain, Sweden, Switzerland, Turkey, the United Kingdom and the United States.

***

TABLE OF CONTENTS

FOREWORD

The examination of manpower policy in Ireland was undertaken by the OECD Manpower and Social Affairs Committee in 1973 at the request of the Irish authorities as the fifteenth in a series of country reviews intended to provide an opportunity for all OECD countries to benefit from each other's experience. As in all such reviews the country being examined reaches an agreement with the specialist examiners appointed by the Organisation on the exact scope of the study and provides them with an explanatory statement of its policy development. These examiners were:

Sir Denis Barnes, then Permanent Secretary of the Department of Employment, London, now Chairman of the Manpower Services Commission;

Mr. R. Broadfield, Senior Economic Adviser in the Dept. of Employment;

Mr. P. Kirstein, Head of Employment Services Branch, Ministry of Labour, Copenhagen, and

Prof. I. Ståhl, Professor of Economics, National Economic Institute, Lund University, Sweden.

In the Irish examination this statement of national policy was later communicated to the Manpower and Social Affairs Committee and is now generally available to those interested on application to the Government Publications Sale Office, GPO Arcade, Dublin 1 (Title: "Manpower Policy in Ireland: Report by the Irish Authorities").

The examiners held a series of discussions in Ireland in 1972 on various aspects of Irish policy with the most important organisations of employers and workers in addition to the various Government and official agencies charged with responsibilities for manpower policy, and members of appropriate university and social research institutes. Based on these discussions and drawing on their own experience, the examiners prepared the report which forms the bulk of the present publication for the Committee. This report was presented to and discussed by the Committee in November 1973 at a meeting attended by representatives of the main national agencies concerned:

Mr. T. O'Carroll, Secretary of the Department of Labour;
Mr. I. Finlay, Assistant Secretary, Department of Labour;
Mr. E. O'Neill, Director, National Manpower Service;
Mr. J. Agnew, Director-General, the Industrial Training Authority;
Mr. J. Dunne, Secretary, Industrial Development Authority;
Mr. P. Kirwan, Principal Officer, Department of Finance.

The conclusions drawn by the Manpower and Social Affairs Committee from these discussions and adopted at a meeting in March 1974 serve as an Introduction to the Examiners' Report.

It will be readily appreciated that the examinations of national manpower policy undertaken by OECD have not been intended to cover all aspects of manpower policy or even to lead to a series of reports with comparable data on identical aspects of policy. The subjects covered have reflected the main concerns of the country examined and the special areas of competence of the examiners. The Irish examination was accordingly largely devoted to a consideration of the strategy for economic development and permanent job creation – as well as to a study of various aspects of the procedures and administrative arrangements adopted to attain these objectives.

Part One

CONCLUSIONS OF THE MANPOWER AND SOCIAL AFFAIRS COMITTEE ON THE EXAMINATION OF MANPOWER POLICY IN IRELAND

CONCLUSIONS OF THE MANPOWER AND SOCIAL AFFAIRS COMMITTEE ON THE EXAMINATION OF MANPOWER POLICY IN IRELAND

INTRODUCTION

The Committee's examination of manpower policy in Ireland has taken place against a background of important structural change, not only in Ireland but also in the interrelationships between Ireland and other countries, especially the EEC countries. These developments, with the further changes flowing from such new factors as the energy crisis, underline the importance to be attached to manpower policy which has a major role to play in ensuring that the adjustments to accommodate the new strains on the economy are made as smoothly as possible. Within Ireland these new strains have resulted in part from the rapid growth of employment in the industrial and service sectors of the economy leading to a considerable movement of population out of the west and into the eastern areas of the country. However, despite these movements, Ireland can still be characterised as a country with considerable reserves of labour in the form of the unemployed and underemployed and a low female participation rate.

That there should be unused manpower resources in a country, together with a tradition of large scale emigration, is not an indictment of its manpower policy or agencies. When such resources remain unused for such a length of time that the explanation can no longer be found in the difficulties of adjusting the available labour supply to the structure of demand, there may be need for greater emphasis on other policies and instruments which are designed to increase capacity and raise the level of demand. In Ireland, even more than in other OECD countries, such an approach involves a consideration of interconnexions with other countries. The most important of these for the Irish economy is the United Kingdom, with which Ireland conducts much of its external trade and to whose capital market it has free access. The nationals of both countries have privileged rights of entry to each other's labour market (although movement to the United Kingdom has been much greater than in the other direction). From the point of view of economic analysis Ireland has displayed some of the characteristics of a regional economy, a point which may be of significance to other countries within the EEC when it comes to discussions on further economic and monetary union.

The process of rapid industrial development is of recent origin. Due to the country's political history, it was only in the thirties that Irish industry began to develop and it was then largely oriented towards the home market. In 1959 the first of the programmes for economic expansion came into effect and a conscious effort was made to strengthen investment, especially in manufacturing industry and agriculture. The development of manpower policy as an accepted instrument of government action followed in the 1960s, although prior to this there had been a number of policies implemented by various Departments and Agencies covering aspects of manpower policy.

The Committee has often had occasion during its examination of national manpower policies to observe that the development of manpower programmes should proceed simultaneously and in co-ordination with the preparation of other plans for economic change. This point has been dealt with in the second and third economic programmes and requires special emphasis as Ireland continues its programmes of accelerated development in an increasingly integrated community.

THE OBJECTIVES OF MANPOWER POLICIES

National manpower policies are directed towards two objectives: on the one hand they seek to provide each individual member of society with the possibility of attaining the situation which he conceived as the most advantageous in terms of personal satisfaction from work and real income; on the other hand they aim at smoothing the course of economic development by promoting the better matching of demand and supply in the labour market. They are thus a part of both economic policy and of social policy in the "welfare" sense of the term. However, this dual role complicates the definition of manpower policy and its reconciliation with demand management policies for example. A further complicating factor is the need for manpower policy to be framed in the light of the best available analysis of the economic situation.

CO-ORDINATION OF GOVERNMENT MACHINERY

These difficulties of definition and reconciliation have repercussions for the composition of the government agencies charged with the design and implementation of manpower policies and for the relationships between these agencies and other organs of government. In most, if not all countries, these relationships are most important when they concern the contribution of manpower policy to discussions and decisions on general economic policy issues.

The Committee attaches special importance to ensuring that, in drawing up macro-economic policy and national budgets, sufficient and timely attention will be paid to the objectives of manpower policy. This usually requires the existence of a Labour Ministry adequately endowed with expertise, information, and resources. The Committee would not wish to make recommendations on precise means of ensuring that adequate attention is paid to manpower aspects of issues. It can, however, state the general requirement that, in the decision-making process, information on the situation and trends of the labour market has to be made available together with analyses and forecasts regarding problems and bottlenecks, and estimates of possible remedial measures. To provide this input is properly within the purview of the arm of government given special responsibility for manpower, and it needs to have adequate resources to be able to achieve this purpose.

A large part of this provision of information and analyses can only be performed if, within the Department of Labour there is a nucleus of staff engaged on work of research and planning to meet various economic contingencies. The Committee accordingly supports the recommendations by the Examiners in this respect, noting that these flow directly from the Council's recommendation on manpower policy. The Committee has also noted with interest that various measures are being developed in different countries to increase the manpower contribution to economic policy discussions (interministerial committees on manpower and employment questions, as in France, or the institution of a rule that a report on manpower consequences has to be produced before measures such as the budget are decided, as in the Netherlands).

Other aspects of economic policy also give rise to comments on co-ordination. Ireland has done more than most countries to promote a policy of industrialisation with a scheme of flexible grants and incentives to encourage firms to settle or expand in Ireland and particularly in the under-developed areas of the country. The objectives of this policy are to provide permanent job opportunities in these areas, to raise the standard of living locally and nationally and to improve the international competitivity of the economy. This policy is developed by the Department of Industry and Commerce and implemented by the Industrial Development Authority and the Shannon Free Airport Development Company. It would seem appropriate that the Department of Labour should have a strong voice in the work of these bodies so as to stress the importance of the employment aspects of their development work.

"HIVING OFF" VERSUS CENTRALISATION

Problems of co-ordination are increased both in number and complexity as the number of units within the government machine increases. A possible way of reducing these problems is to reduce the number of units. Sometimes this can be done by merger, but another approach is to "hive off" various services to subsidiaries under the general guidance of a Central Government Department. When this takes place the "hived off" service is given a degree of autonomy provided that it follows the guidance given by its parent Ministry and keeps within the budget allocated to it on the recommendation of the Ministry.

The criterion which has been put forward by the Devlin Committee in Ireland for deciding whether or not to hive off a service is whether or not the function is one of policy-making or of policy execution. The first is considered to be an essential prerogative of central government. Executive services could be removed from the government service when this could be seen to be in the public interest because of the advantages resulting from:

(*a*) greater flexibility in expenditure within approved budgets;

(*b*) greater freedom to develop services to meet the needs of the "customers";

(*c*) possibility of recruiting staff otherwise than as permanent civil servants;

(*d*) freedom from complex procedures arising from detailed parliamentary control.

In the areas covered by this review of manpower policy there are two services which are fully hived off – the Industrial Development Authority (with SFADCO as its agent for the mid-West region) and AnCO, the Industrial Training Authority – and one which has some degree of autonomy, the National Manpower Service (NMS), but which remains within the Department of Labour. The advantages in establishing the IDA as an independent agency (although subject to some strict financial controls) are evidently that this facilitates negotiations with potential employers and speeds decisions on making incentives available. A possible disadvantage is that the IDA might be so large and experienced in its own area that the supervisory Ministry has difficulty in exercising its role as policy-maker. For AnCO an advantage it derives from its status is that it is more easily able to discuss firms' training problems and advise them if it is outside the government machine. The fact that its controlling council is tripartite must be of advantage in securing general acceptance of its policies. It would also hope to benefit from being able to recruit staff on terms comparable to those found in industry. Given the close interconnexions between the work of NMS and AnCO there are disadvantages in not giving the NMS the same degree of autonomy, a point which the Irish authorities are considering as the NMS gradually expands to its full operating strength.

The Committee considers that Irish experience with "hiving off" is instructive for those countries which have not yet created this form of administrative structure or have not been satisfied with results. To some extent the undoubted achievements of both the IDA and AnCO can be attributed to the resources made available for what have been recognised as high priority objectives. But a part at least of this success can also be attributed to the flexible approach which hived off agencies can adopt.

An aspects of this process to which the Committee suggests particular attention should be given is the organisation of hived off services at the local level. It must, of course, be understood that functionally hived off services ordinarily have regional organisations which co-ordinate their work within the individual regions. In Ireland the IDA, AnCO and NMS have regional offices which co-operate formally in various committees and also informally. The issue is whether this form of co-ordination is the most effective or whether devolution of a wide range of executive powers to a regional body is a better approach. SFADCO has some features of such a service within the Shannon Airport area. Other examples can be found in countries such as Sweden where the regional labour market organisation has responsibilities for a wide variety of measures to correct imbalances on the labour market by temporary and permanent job creation as well as by measures to adapt labour supply. The trend in the United States to make states and cities the vehicle for designing and delivering manpower programmes can also be viewed in the same light.

THE ROLE OF THE SOCIAL PARTNERS

The Committee has always recognised the need to ensure that problems of co-ordination with the social partners are resolved at an early stage in the elaboration and application of manpower policies. There are evident advantages in ensuring that their legitimate interests are safeguarded so that unnecessary discussion and opposition are avoided. There is also the point that by generating debate with the social partners at an early stage it is possible to focus on the basic issues and long-term objectives of policy.

Ireland has been at least partially successful in its attempts to develop satisfactory means of consultation as far as AnCO is concerned. Its tripartite representation at sector and local levels appears to have helped to secure general recognition of the importance of training in Irish management and labour circles. The IDA, which reports to the Ministry of Industry and Commerce, rather than to the Minister of Labour, has so far managed with less formal contacts with the representatives of organised labour. As regards the whole range of economic and social policy, the Irish authorities are making efforts to secure a greater sense of commitment on the part of the social partners and a better opportunity for discussion of objectives and means of attaining them, through their representation on the National Economic and Social Council which has recently been established by the Government (replacing the defunct National Economic Council).

The Committee considers that in order to obtain the required degree of co-operation and understanding, it will often be necessary to entrust the social partners with greater responsibilities than simply providing advice or acquiescing in initiatives taken by government. Accordingly, it welcomes the action now being taken to provide a forum where employment problems can be related to other economic and social problems and solutions can be sought.

THE INSTRUMENTS OF MANPOWER POLICY

So far these conclusions have been concerned with the organisational framework for the implementation of manpower policy. Now it is appropriate to consider some of the ways in which manpower policy has been implemented in Ireland.

PERMANENT JOB CREATION

The White Paper on Manpower Policy stated that "the steps taken by the Government to promote economic growth in all sectors of the economy have, as one of their primary aims, the attainment and maintenance of employment on the highest levels practicable". The second and third economic and social development programmes also stressed the priority of enabling all who wish to achieve their full potential in work to do so. The main brunt of employment-creation activity has, of course, been borne by the IDA which has been provided with greater resources than all other manpower policy agents together.

Although unemployment has always persisted in the country, the IDA has not supported plans for labour-intensive industrial development indiscriminately, for this would have accentuated the population and industrial imbalance – too much in the east, especially round Dublin, in relation to the west. So the IDA has developed a flexible scheme of grants in which a number of factors are taken into account including: number of jobs to be created both directly and indirectly; their quality; the stability of employment; contribution to exports; and dependence upon raw materials available in Ireland. Three main criticisms can in principle be levelled against such a highly flexible scheme. First, despite its flexibility, until recently it has concentrated on encouraging *industrial* development on the basis that creation of service employment would follow more or less automatically. Services can, however, offer considerable possibilities of good-quality labour-intensive employment in such fields as data-processing. Second, the emphasis on factors such as the contribution to exports and dependence on Irish raw materials may distract attention from the primary aim which is to make full use of (to quote the third Programme) "the nation's richest and most diverse asset" – its people. It could be argued that a regionally and, if necessary, occupationally differentiated scheme of employment premiums might, for a given injection of funds, lead to a greater incentive to increase employment. The third main criticism related to the possibility that a very flexible scheme could give potential employers scope for resorting to strategems and pressures to maximise their scale of grants.

The Committee has been impressed with the defence of the Irish authorities that, despite the theoretical force of these criticisms, the second and third at least are largely inappropriate in the Irish context. It also notes that the IDA are now taking measures to encourage service employment in Ireland. The Irish authorities have contended that the first criterion taken into account in assessing eligibility for grant is a realistic estimate of the number of jobs to be created. Only when this has been agreed is there any consideration of the various other factors which are acknowledged to be important. Grants are made refundable if the estimate of employment to be created turns out to be inaccurate. As part of the measures to prevent employers using undue pressure to obtain favourable terms, the approval of the Government has to be obtained before aid can be granted in excess of £350,000.

The advantages which have been claimed for a system of capital grants rather than an employment subsidy can be summarised as follows:

- capital grants, being fixed, once-for-all sums, are attractive to the potential employer because of the initial liquidity they provide at the start of his operations and their clear-cut financial nature;
- employment subsidies, to be effective need to be given on a continuing basis (e.g. 7 years in the United Kingdom, two and a half years in the Swedish scheme) and can become an open-ended commitment.

The advantages of an employment subsidy are:

- the subsidy can be varied to encourage the employment of specific groups of employees such as trainees, older workers, handicapped persons, or employment in specific industries or occupations;

- because the subsidy is not a once-for-all payment but is given over a long period, it can be expected to stabilise employment in the recipient firms at a higher level with consequent multiplier effects in the whole surrounding region;
- an employment subsidy is an incentive to an existing firm to increase employment and output using its existing plant more intensively; and to a business whose capital requirements are low.

The Committee has noted that Ireland is one of a growing number of countries using a scheme of capital grants based primarily on the expected employment effect. Obviously different methods can be used to create employment for special groups or special areas. The Committe suggests that all countries review the appropriateness of traditional schemes in the light of changing circumstances and new experiences in various countries working with different methods of stimulating employment and development.

EDUCATION AND TRAINING

The Committee wishes in this connexion to recall that its examination of manpower policy has not been comprehensive; a selection of topics has had to be made for reasons of good management of resources and the need to complete the examination whilst its findings are relevant to current problems. For these reasons and because relationships between the education system and employment (and employment-oriented services) are to be the usbject of extensive work in OECD in the near future, the Committee will confine itself to some general comments on this fundamental problem. One of these is the fact that the relationship between education and employment is a general problem within most, if not all, countries hence the importance it assumes within OECD. As regards relations between education and training, efforts at reforming or modernising the one must be accompanied by development of the other. This requires exchanges of plans and experiences between the different agencies concerned so as to achieve a reconciliation of policies and programmes. The same is true as concerns the relation between efforts and methods in the development of education and training programmes for youth and for adults.

MANAGEMENT TRAINING

The need for an active manpower policy emanates to a great extent from the fact that manpower does not respond speedily to changes in market conditions. The reasons for this can be found partly in inherent differences in natural capacities, partly in temperament and scale of values, partly in lack of information, costs of moving house or acquiring adequate skills, but also in acquired skills and habits which are difficult to change. The fact that prior to the passage of the Industrial Training Act in 1967 Irish firms were reckoned not to be doing sufficient training, is a reminder that the slowness in reaction to market changes referred to above applies as much to employers as to employees and points to the important place occupied by management training in an endeavour to increase the rate of economic development.

Obviously the need for this form of training is greater in a country where the average size of firm is small and where industrial development is largely of recent origin. The 1967 Industrial Training Act entrusts overall responsibility for training at all levels in industry and commerce to AnCO, but it is the Irish Management Institute which, in practice, provides management courses. As the Institute is controlled and largely financed by independent businessmen and firms it is evident that there could be possibilities for differences in priorities between it and AnCO. Close co-operation will continue to be needed to ensure that the standard of management training keeps pace with the rising needs of the whole economy, especially its most rapidly expanding sectors (without, of course, mushrooming into a growth industry in its own right, as has threatened to happen in some countries).

INDUSTRIAL TRAINING

AnCO encourages firms' industrial training efforts through a system of levies and grants differentiated by broad industrial sectors. This is similar to the system adopted in the United Kingdom with the Industrial Training Boards and has the advantage that it makes firms in the industries subject to the levies anxious to provide a satisfactory level of training if they wish to obtain the refund of their levy.

As long as the expectation of higher productivity as a consequence of a better trained staff is an inadequate incentive on its own to employers, some system of grants or subsidies will be needed. This could be financed either out of general taxation or by a differentiated tax on an industry's wage bill. The Committee suggests for consideration that while the levy/grant system is still a useful weapon it may not be altogether appropriate in its present form as a technique for financing the long-term solution to Ireland's industrial training needs for the following reasons:

(*a*) small firms are exempt from levy because of the additional administrative burden it imposes on them and on AnCO (though they may "opt in" voluntarily) yet small firms employ a high proportion of the non-agricultural labour force;

(*b*) after levy/grant's initial salutary shock has worn off it may tend to be regarded by employers as an example of well-intentioned but misguided government interference and lead to a hardening of attitudes against AnCO's efforts to provide a training guidance service.

In addition to the levy/grant system of encouraging training, AnCO also operates its own training centres (9 at the end of 1973 with an annual through-put in the region of 3,000 trainees) at which apprentices can be given a first year of off-the-job training and adult workers can be trained for a variety of semi-skilled occupations. After long negotiations with the unions, agreement has been reached to begin training at one centre up to skilled level. There is an ambitious programme to treble the number of training places and reduce the length of courses so that by 1977/8 through-put of trainees will have almost quadrupled. The Committee endorses this dual approach to the problem of increasing the output of trainees and points out that the application of employment subsidies to trainees already referred to above, may enable a reduction in the length of training courses to be more readily accepted by employers.

The need for more but shorter training is underlined by a number of factors which, although common to most countries, are of particular importance in Ireland:

- until now the numbers leaving agriculture have not been matched by those availing themselves of training courses. Many have emigrated rather than seek alternative work or undergo training at home. As it is an objective of government policy to reduce involuntary emigration, there will be a need to design courses which will enable these persons to make a smooth transition out of agriculture;
- as industrialisation develops in importance to the national economy and in technological content, the need for training will increase in old and new skills;
- government policy also seeks to increase the opportunities for women to participate in economic life to a greater extent than hitherto (Irish female participation rates being amongst the lowest in OECD countries) but the number of women being trained by AnCO centres remains very small. Relatively short training courses would be attractive to them;
- existing apprenticeship schemes are of long duration in relation to the level of skill aimed at. For this and other reasons they are unlikely to be satisfactory as a sole source of supply of the skills needed by the expanding economy. The institution of shorter training courses for adults would strengthen the arguments in favour of a parallel reduction in length of apprenticeship;
- ready availability of trained workers can be as important an inducement to a firm thinking of establishing or expanding in Ireland as capital grants.

Various aspects of Irish training schemes can be pointed out for study of their possible relevance in other countries:

1. training centre programmes can be geared to the particular needs of individual companies in addition to the needs of industry as a whole. Under this scheme trainees are released for special courses in AnCO centres, and are paid wages by the employer during training. The employer also pays AnCO the costs it has incurred;
2. Mobile training units have been set up to provide short courses in areas affected by redundancies and unemployment. Six units with a limited capacity (180 places) were being operated by the end of 1973;
3. persons who are not up to the educational standard for existing courses have been given the opportunity to undertake short induction courses to bring them up to this standard (1,500 people attended special courses of this type in the summer of 1973);
4. from July 1973 the scale of allowances of trainees was increased to give them a substantial lead over those on unemployment benefit.

THE EMPLOYMENT SERVICE

The NMS is in the process of being established to provide a high-quality placement service. To do this it needs adequate resources and the co-operation of all other agents operating in the manpower field, especially employers and employees. Because demand for labour is not evenly spread throughout the country it has seemed wise to develop the service gradually, starting from those centres where its value could be most easily demonstrated in terms of cutting down the time spent in looking for suitable jobs and improving the selection of candidates offered to an employer.

Placement cannot be developed as a service on its own; it has to be accompanied by other activities if the NMS is to fulfil its role as a manpower agency serving individuals and contributing to national economic development. It must therefore provide a national vocational guidance and counselling service which in turn presupposes the possibility of assessing the customer's needs and relating them to good information about actual, and forecasts of potential, developments on the labour market. The provision of these is partly a question of contacts and co-ordination with other bodies such as AnCO and the IDA, and partly a question of resources to obtain the necessary basic information. The NMS is making use of its staff in the regions to obtain some of this information, a course of action, which also increases their possibilities of contacting employers and winning their confidence. But this is not likely to lead to a very consistent coverage of all aspects of employment and the Committee suggests that it may be necessary to devise additional sources of information. More important than that is the need for the NMS to have access to a research and planning unit, which could be charged with analyses of tendencies and forecasts of developments on the labour market so that the strategies and priorities of all manpower agencies can be adequately co-ordinated.

The Committee's examination of Irish manpower policy has shown that it is being used to support economic development chiefly through measures to stimulate demand for labour by the industrial development programme and to improve supply through the encouragement of training and the provision of an improved employment service. At this stage of the country's development it seems that greater resources now need to be devoted to strengthening the machinery for planning and co-ordinating these efforts and for preparing for the problems which will arise as Ireland progresses towards a state of full employment. Pleas for increased resources are likely to be best received by Government (and the public generally) when assurance can be given that they will in fact have a high pay-off for the economy. This indicates a need for further public discussion and explanation of the role of manpower policy.

Part Two

EXAMINERS' REPORT

I

ECONOMIC BACKGROUND AND THE ROLE OF MANPOWER POLICY

GENERAL PROBLEMS OF LABOUR MARKET POLICY

1.1 As an introduction to our examination of the main objectives and operation of Irish manpower policies it is appropriate to consider some general features of manpower policy as a background to the discussion of our report in the OECD. The reason for certain economic policies of governments – including manpower policies – in a market economy where the allocation of goods, services and factors of production is determined by the price mechanism, is that governments aim to modify or compensate for the results which would follow in the absence of government intervention. Government economic policy can thus be evaluated in terms of the objective of adjusting or compensating for what might be described as different types of market "failure".

1.2 A basic problem in identifying the market "failures" towards which labour market policies are directed is the extent to which labour and other markets in goods, services and factors of production are inter-related. As the labour market occupies a central position in any economy – with labour as a primary factor of production typically generating about 75% of the total value of production – it is obvious that failures in the labour market will have a serious impact on the functioning of the economy as a whole. Conversely labour market policies will have a great influence on economic variables relevant to a broad macro-economic policy framework. Labour market policies can be used to alleviate problems such as unemployment which may not be caused by structural failures in the labour market.

1.3 The market failures of significance in relation to the labour market policies can be divided into two main groups. The first group embraces the problems of instability at the macro-economic level, related to uncertainty and expectations in the goods, factor and credit markets and the downward inflexibility of money wages. The second group of problems concerns the internal working of the labour market which is characterised by special features such as heterogeneity – a circumstance which creates high transaction costs and would lead one to expect a theoretically imperfect pricing and allocation situation. The creation of employment services and similar organisations, aids to training and mobility are attempts to overcome this transaction cost problem and to alleviate the lack of information, uncertainty and financial problems which prevent the achievement of optimal individual investment in human capital. These two types of market failure to a certain extent correspond to another distinction often used in the analysis of labour market problems, namely the unemployment created by overall demand deficiency and unemployment created by structural factors.

1.4 A theoretical analysis of causes of the imperfect functioning of the labour market is vital for the selection of appropriate policy measures. Where the basic problem is one of deficient general demand, the appropriate policies are economic measures such as increased Government or private expenditure via changes in tax rates or the money supply or possible exchange rate adjustments. If the imperfect working of the labour market is primarily due to structural causes, general measures of this kind will tend to intensify pressures in already tight sub-markets without having significant effects on unemployment in the depressed areas or occupations. The appropriate remedies for these structural problems will be selective measures such as retraining or relocation of the work-force to specific areas or activities.

1.5 This distinction between the role of general economic or manpower policies is widely used in the debate about general versus selective manpower measures. It is necessary to set out these principles as a preliminary to analysing the use of manpower policy in a particular national environment in order to deal with key issues such as whether permanently high unemployment is explained by structural or general causes and hence whether highly selective measures are really the appropriate policy measures or primarily a substitute for inadmissible or unpopular general measures.

1.6 Before moving on to the specific characteristics of the Irish economy, one further aspect of the use of general and selective measures should be mentioned. By definition, general measures, such as interest rate changes, treat all firms or individuals equally, whereas selective measures, such as individually determined training grants, are discriminatory in the sense that individuals and firms are not treated equally. A discriminatory policy may be judged necessary to achieve desired goals, but it will inevitably cause administrative problems as considerable room is left for bargaining and negotiation between firms (and individuals) and Government authorities.

THE BACKGROUND TO IRISH MANPOWER POLICY

1.7 The preceding discussion of the potential use of manpower policies for the alleviation of imbalances in the labour market forms a back-cloth on which to identify the principal characteristics of the Irish labour market and comment on the scope for the use of active manpower policies to deal with Irish manpower problems.

1.8 An outstanding feature of the Irish labour market has been the relatively high level of unemployment – as measured by the live register – over the last decade. Table 1 below summarises the relevant data:

Table 1. LABOUR FORCE AND UNEMPLOYMENT IN IRELAND
1961-1971

	1961	1966	1971
Labour force (thousand)	1,090.2	1,110.6	1,133.3
Number unemployed (thousand)	55.6	52.2	68.0
Rate of unemployment (per cent)	5.1	4.7	6.0

The use of a live register system for estimating the size of the potential labour force rather than the labour force survey method, will tend to underestimate the numbers of women and young people and perhaps introduce an upward bias for older men due to the requirement to register in order to receive unemployment benefit. A study of participation rates for women confirms the impression that there is a considerable untapped pool of potential female labour in Ireland. In 1966 the participation rate for married women was 5.3%, and a similar estimate for all women between the ages of 14 and 64 would indicate a participation rate slightly above 30%, compared with about 50% for a country such as Sweden. Special features of the Irish family situation such as the large number of children per family and the importance accorded to a woman's role in the home – explain this phenomenon in part, but the low participation of married women in job opportunities is probably also explained by the severe employment situation as well as traditional moral and social values. There is evidence also of underemployment in the agricultural sector which employs about 25% of the labour force but contributes only 15% of total GNP.

1.9 A second feature of the Irish labour market is the continuing high level of emigration. During the period 1961-71, net emigration from Ireland totalled 130,000 persons, most of whom went to the United Kingdom. Emigration has taken place mainly from the 19 to 24 age group, leaving a low percentage of the domestic population in the active age groups. There were no legal obstacles to mobility between Ireland and the United Kingdom throughout this period, and the fluctuations in emigrant flows which have occurred appear to result largely from changes in the employment situation in the United Kingdom. Thus the decrease in emigration in 1972 was probably due to the then depressed employment conditions in the United Kingdom.

1.10 The problem of Irish emigration is often discussed in terms of voluntary vs. involuntary migration. Although the terms are far from precise they are similar to a "pull" and "push" concept. Migration of the pull type is caused by wage differentials between employment in two areas sufficient to compensate for direct mobility costs and other costs of an invisible or intangible character for the individual. Push effects are connected with a situation where remaining in an area means continuous unemployment or a high risk of future unemployment. With a high rate of unemployment relative to the receiving region or country the push effects will tend to predominate.

1.11 A decrease in unemployment rates will decrease the push effects. Even in a case in which a decrease in unemployment is accompanied by a decrease in relative wages, i.e. increasing real wage differentials, compared with the receiving country, it is probable that the decrease in "push"-emigration is more than sufficient to compensate for a simultaneous increase in incentives for migration of the pull-type. A feature of the Irish emigration pattern which is often discussed is the fact that migration often goes directly from the depressed areas to employment abroad. The pull effect from domestic areas with lower unemployment is not sufficient to compensate for the still stronger pull effect say from the British labour market. This type of migration in "long jumps" is a not uncommon phenomenon in much international migration. For a long time the pull effects of the Swedish manufacturing industry belt in mid-Sweden have been stronger than the pull effects from South Finland in determining the movement of redundant workers from North Finland. As soon as the migrant is ready to accept the costs of mobility – including intangibles – one can expect the differences in pull effects to be decisive; especially when the social environment, (language, school system, the probability of meeting relatives etc.) does not differ very much between employment abroad or employment at home in an area of relatively high labour demand.

1.12 A large-scale emigration is closely connected with two somewhat different problems of "vicious circles" affecting the Irish economy. As was stated above it is necessary to decrease unemployment to stop emigration of the push type. But this is not generally consistent with immediate increase in net real wages. An increase in employment can either be created by devaluation (thus decreasing real wages for those already employed) or by increasing economic growth which presupposes increased investment and a higher savings ratio and a tendency in the short run to a decreased growth (and in extreme cases an absolute decrease) in net real wages. A decrease in push effects will consequently increase incentives of the pull type. Under favourable conditions one can hope that the decrease in push effects more than offsets the increased pull effects.

1.13 The second "vicious circle" involves depopulation or long-term decreases in population and the difficulties of exploiting economies of scale in the provision of facilities and opportunities for the individual. This problem may occur on a local basis with difficulties in offering services in sectors with high fixed costs and on a nation-wide basis with too small an internal market for domestic production. A fall in population and consequently in facilities will in itself create expectations of future decreases; expectations which easily become self-fulfilling.

1.14 The third outstanding feature of the Irish labour market is the relationship between the Irish and United Kingdom economies which has already been referred to in connection with the emigration problem. The relationship has more far-reaching ramifications than have been discussed to date, however, as observation suggests that the two economies demonstrate many features of an inter-regional rather than an international character. Not only are the two labour markets closely related, Irish and United Kingdom pounds have traditionally maintained a parity relationship. This situation which exists for economic and monetary purposes makes it unlikely that independent exchange rate adjustment will be included in the range of Irish macro-economic policies, and this may place a greater burden on alternative economic and manpower policy measures. The fact that the economic relationship between Ireland and the United Kingdom is only partial in that the two countries pursue separate domestic and international policies has also meant that Ireland has not been able to benefit from the substantial transfers that occur via taxation, social and regional policies between high and low income regions of a single national economy. On the other hand it does give Ireland more freedom to pursue economic and fiscal policies which it conceives as suited to its own special needs.

1.15 The three main features discussed here – high unemployment, emigration and the relationship between the Irish and United Kingdom economies – are of obvious importance in discussing the scope for manpower policy in Ireland. Are the observed imbalances of such a type that highly selective and discriminatory policy measures really are the right policies or are the imbalances of such a fundamental kind that manpower policy will treat only the symptoms rather than the causes? Before going on to a more detailed examination of the different programmes in Irish manpower policy it is necessary to discuss this important and critical question.

1.16 An alternative formulation of the problem would be to consider whether "deficient-demand" (together with some constraints on admissible policies) is a stronger explaining factor of the Irish situation than internal, structural conditions in the labour market. Still another way of formulating the problem would be to conceive of a hypothetical economic policy in which internal demand was substantially increased with the objective of stimulating investment and reducing unemployment. What would be the consequences for wages and prices, employment in different sectors and areas and the balance of payments?

1.17 It is reasonable to assume that an internal demand increase would decrease unemployment, but as there are substantial imbalances between regions and sectors there is a high risk of creating shortages in already rather tight sectors causing wage drift and inflationary price movements. There will thus be a price to pay for the reduced unemployment in the slack areas or sectors. However, it would be possible to combine a general increase in demand with selective devices such as an employment tax or premium differentiated between regions, say with a positive tax on employment in the Dublin area and an employment premium in the west of Ireland.

1.18 An increase of internal demand would also tend to increase imports and discourage exports, thus increasing the deficit on the balance of payments. Up to a certain point this would be no problem as long as Irish pounds are accepted equally with British pounds at the existing exchange rate. To a very high degree the possibility of being successful with a general demand-increasing policy is dependent on what occurs simultaneously in the United Kingdom; as long as the Irish inflation rate does not exceed the British no fundamental problems will arise.

1.19 It is also possible that the increased demand would exert such great pressures on the Irish pound that it would be difficult to maintain parity with the British pound. This does not in theory exclude the possibility of achieving a higher employment level and fuller utilisation of capacity. A devaluation might in itself be a sufficient measure (together with measures alleviating internal structural imbalances); imports would fall, export incentives would be increased and employment levels raised to a new equilibrium. We are not advocating a complete changeover from selective to general policies, because the issues involved in Ireland are too complex for such a simple situation. However, a discussion of hypothetical policy alternatives may illustrate how much of the problems of unemployment and imbalance really are problems suitably treated by manpower policies or similar selective measures (e.g. the subsidisation of new firms within the comprehensive regional policy) and how much they require the application of more general measures.

1.20 The key issues are whether the Irish problem of deficient productive capacity and entrepreneurship would be alleviated by a more expansive general demand plus selective action policy and what the consequences of this policy would be for the rate of domestic inflation. The problem of deficient capacity and enterprise may result from a combination of insufficient general incentives to investment and inadequate manpower policies. The policies which currently form the basis of Irish development strategy attempt to overcome the problem by creating highly specific incentives which, while provided on the same basis to Irish and foreign entrepreneurs, have mainly been made use of by foreign firms. In our view the type of enterprise attracted by this policy will not provide a long-term basis for Irish economic development, in that its attributes will be related to the nature of the incentive, rather than the character of the Irish economy and often the decision-making centre will be located abroad. Our view of the Irish problem is that inadequate domestic and external demand for Irish goods and services has limited the incentive for the exercise of domestic investment.

1.21 Inflation is already a serious problem in Ireland, with the rate of increase in the consumer price index exceeding 9 % in 1971 and 1972. A greater emphasis on broad macro-economic measures to improve the historically poor growth performance of the Irish economy might further intensify these inflationary pressures and it would seem necessary for the successful application of these policies that a firmer grip should be taken on the trend of prices in the country. The Employer/Labour Conference has made two national wage agreements, but these appear to have achieved no more than stabilising the rate of inflation at a relatively high level. The possible combination of more radical demand and exchange rate policies and the current attempts to reduce the rate of inflation in the United Kingdom, suggest that the Irish Government needs to take a more positive role in income determination with the objective of significantly reducing the rate of inflation.

REGIONS AND SECTORS – IMBALANCE AND DEVELOPMENT

1.22 The Irish economy has very large potential labour force reserves, especially if the attitudes towards and among women change in the longer term and if emigration decreases (paragraphs 1.8–1.13). There are large potential benefits also in the transfer of labour from low-productivity sectors to sectors (or even regions) with a higher productivity. This transfer has been considerable during the last decade with a decrease of about 100,000 persons, in the agricultural sectors and a substantial increase in the non-agricultural ones. At the same time the ex-post savings ratio has increased from 13 % to 23 %, representing a considerable increase in the resources available for investment.

1.23 There are significant imbalances in unemployment. In the table below unemployment rates are given for the 10 largest towns in order to indicate the existence of permanent imbalance.

Table 2. UNEMPLOYMENT RATES IN 10 LARGEST TOWNS

Town	Gainfully occupied persons in census 1966(1)	Average number on live register as percentage of (1)			
		1967	1968	1969	1970
1. Dublin	231,900	5.3	5.5	5.3	6.1
2. Cork	44,800	5.0	4.8	4.3	4.3
3. Limerick	20,300	8.6	7.4	6.8	8.1
4. Dun Laoghaire	19,900	4.2	4.4	4.6	5.1
5. Waterford	11,400	6.1	5.7	6.8	6.8
6. Galway	9,400	3.5	3.4	3.6	4.1
7. Dundalk	8,000	10.1	8.9	7.7	8.2
8. Drogheda	7,400	11.8	11.7	10.3	11.4
9. Bray	4,900	6.6	7.7	8.0	8.4
10. Sligo	4,700	6.3	6.4	6.0	6.8

These towns have roughly a little more than one-third of the total employment and slightly above 40 % of all non-agricultural employment. Unemployment with respect to industrial sectors shows a similar picture.

Table 3. AVERAGE UNEMPLOYMENT RATES BY INDUSTRY

	1961-1965	1966-1970
Total unemployed as percent of insured persons	6.2	7.3
of which:		
Agriculture	9.2	13.6
Mining and Quarrying	5.6	6.7
Manufacturing	4.1	5.1
Construction	12.6	14.1
Electricity, Gas and Water	3.8	4.3
Commerce	4.5	5.4
Transport	8.6	8.9
Services	4.1	4.6
Other	15.7	20.5

1.24 Table 3 indicates, together with Table 3 in the Irish Authorities' report, substantial differences between sectors. The unemployment rate in the construction industry has been between 12 and 15 % while it is generally around or below 5 % in the manufacturing sector. Also striking is the relative stability of the unemployment figures over time; although to a certain degree this may just be mirroring the measurement method. It is generally known that unemployment measured by regular labour force surveys or measurements of changes in participation rates shifts more quickly than live register data would indicate.

1.25 The constancy of labour market imbalances – seen either in a regional or in a sectoral perspective – could be a strong argument for "structural" explanations, and in consequence for structurally oriented and selective measures to cope with pockets of permanently high unemployment for which general demand management measures would probably not be adequate. But although some part of the high unemployment can be looked upon as a kind of transitional unemployment in a country in transition from an agricultural to an industrial economy, the general levels seem to be high enough to suggest the need for measures of general demand-management character; and the constancy of the imbalances, support of this policy with selective or discriminatory measures.

1.26 To a certain extent the situation is paradoxical: the Irish labour market shows a high degree of mobility regarding emigration while internal and occupational mobility is not sufficient to reduce constant imbalances over time. One part of the explanation might be rigidities in wages and a wage-structure with inadequate regional differentials, which supports an uneven distribution of unemployment originally created by the transition and development process.* Another explanation may be the obstacles to occupational mobility, as recruitment to different skilled trades is largely via the apprenticeship system, and there may be severe difficulties in a flexible occupational choice for individuals above the younger age groups. A highly compartmentalised or segmented labour market will always show these tendencies of structural unemployment.

1.27 Another striking feature of the Irish economy which may be of some importance for understanding the Irish growth problem is the corporate structure and the distribution of firms between different industries. The largest firms are to be found in traditional industries – e.g. food and beverages, cement, construction – while there are few or no firms of international size in new industries. To a high degree industrial development policy has had the effect of attracting subsidiaries of foreign companies to open operations in Ireland. Somewhat simplifying one could say that there are few firms or corporations with a high internal growth potential (as regards employment) in the Irish economy. Probably this lack of growing firms with returns to scale and significant research and development programmes is of greatest importance in the manufacturing sector.**

1.28 One exogenous factor is of great importance for the future development of the Irish economy: Irish membership of the European Economic Community. Membership of the EEC will lead to substantially higher prices and incomes for the agricultural sector, thus providing a basis for further growth, and might be expected to reduce the dependance of Ireland on the British economy. Entry will, however, bring problems as well as benefits. With the removal of tariff barriers, Ireland will be exposed to competition from the Community's large industrial enterprises. Some of the characteristics of the historical economic relationship with the United King-

* The obvious assumption is that at any time there exists a wage-structure between occupations, industries and regions that will keep unemployment down to a minimum determined by transitions and frictions (at a given level of general demand).

** It is here possible to compare with the industrial structure of some other small countries like Switzerland with large international firms in pharmaceuticals (e.g. Geigy), Netherlands (Philips in electronics, Shell in oil) and Sweden (with Volvo, Asea, Atlas Copco, Alfa Laval, all in manufacturing).

dom will simply be created on a larger scale. The current rate of Irish inflation will be a major problem as Irish exports will prove increasingly uncompetitive and imports from other EEC countries more attractive. Ireland will lose its position as an attractive location for European companies wishing to sell on the United Kingdom market which have previously been able to take advantage of the Anglo-Irish Free Trade Agreement by establishing subsidiaries in Ireland. A wider horizon will also be opened to Irish emigrants, which may intensify the drain of young, qualified manpower. The challenge to Irish economic and manpower policies presented by EEC entry is thus considerable, and a more radical and ambitious range of policies seems to be necessary to meet this challenge.

REGIONAL POLICY

1.29 In the preceding paragraphs the regional imbalances in the Irish economy were described. Without actually weighting the different factors it is possible to explain the imbalances starting from technological development phasing out employment in agriculture and traditional sectors. This structurally determined unemployment is for various reasons not absorbed: rigid wage rates, too little regional wage differentiation and slow occupational mobility reinforce the imbalances. The negative cumulative effect in the declining areas is another reinforcing factor, and insufficient job creation nation-wide intensifies the problem.

1.30 The main regional policies carried through in Ireland in response to these problems are of two different but interrelated types:

(*a*) Regional development plans providing a general framework for development. The idea behind these plans could be formulated as an attempt to counter the negative effects of decline and provide common forward plans for government authorities and private investors for regions and towns where growth is expected. The regional development plans attempt, by use of indicative planning techniques, to solve the very difficult problem of interdependent investment decisions without going over to direct investment and localised controls. If these declarations are to have a fair chance of being believed and actively supported by private investors it will be necessary to be seen to create the required infrastructure: in the manpower field this means adequate training facilities and a well functioning manpower service.

(*b*) The second arm of regional policy is the operation of the semi-independent development corporations, IDA and SFAD Co; the first operating over the whole country, the other limited to the Shannon area in the West. Both authorities offer incentives to newly established firms: complete exemption for 15 years from taxes on profits derived abroad, different types of grants towards the cost of fixed assets or research and development, and training grants. Tax relief on increased exports and fixed asset grants are also offered to existing enterprises. All the grants are negotiable up to certain limits – 50 % of the approved cost in the designated areas in the west and 35 % in the rest of the country.

1.31 This grant system can be looked upon as a discriminatory subsidy to specific industries in certain areas. Two main problems seem to arise. If the main problem is labour surplus there are arguments for compensating directly for the differences between actual wages and some kind of equilibrium wage (the latter being lower) than to give subsidies for capital equipment. Without detailed control there will be a tendency for capital subsidies to create a bias towards more capital intensive projects. The expansion effect of the subsidies is thus partly offset by a capital increase and labour saving effect. To avoid these effects, however, the grants are limited to new projects and the rate for the grant is partly dependent on the employment effect (after individual negotiation). Of the 600 projects assisted over the period 1960–71, one-third were in Irish-owned firms and the rest in foreign-owned firms. The share of new employment from projects in foreign-owned firms was still higher – about 75 %. The grant system has thus significantly affected the corporation structure by mainly promoting foreign subsidiaries. The long-term problems of the corporation structure which are intensified by this policy, have been mentioned earlier.

1.32 A possible revision of the regional development grants might be towards measures which are neutral between different types of firms – certainly designed so as not to provide a greater incentive to incoming foreign firms than to developments in established firms seeking to move into new sectors – and measures that directly promote more labour-intensive projects. It would also be an advantage if the scope for individual negotiations could be decreased and less discriminatory measures could be used.

1.33 One measure of this type – directly related to the fact that wages show little inter-regional variation despite varying regional employment levels – is a regionally differentiated employment tax or subsidy; e.g. with a positive tax *per capita* (or a percentage of the wage bill) in Dublin and a corresponding subsidy in the West. This measure could in principle be self-financing with the tax rate dependent upon the long-term unemployment rate in the area. A measure of this kind which is not negotiable on an individual or on a project basis – is also neutral towards different sectors and between export promotion and imports substitution.*

* The export bias in the development grant system is another indication that currency problems may have been a factor behind manpower problems in Ireland.

II

MANPOWER POLICIES AND THE ROLE OF THE DEPARTMENT OF LABOUR

THE ROLE OF THE DEPARTMENT OF LABOUR IN GENERAL MANPOWER POLICY

2.1 There are two basic requirements for effective manpower policies. First the policies should be consistent with the economic objectives outlined in Chapter IV of the Irish Authorities' Report and meet the requirements of the policies developed by the Government to achieve these objectives. There must be effective organisation to secure this, though it may not in practice be easy to establish. Secondly there should be clear responsibility for the execution or operation of manpower policies through appropriate organisations and institutions.

2.2 Arrangements for co-ordination of manpower policies with general economic policies are bound to focus round the point of responsibility in Government for the financing of basic Government operations and the "management" of the economy. In Ireland this point is the Department of Finance. At the same time, responsibility for the execution and development of manpower policies should (as with other Government policies in particular areas) be the concern of a Department with the necessary knowledge and expertise. The Department of Labour in Ireland was established for this reason and in order to make policy in the fields of industrial relations and safety, health and welfare of workers.

2.3 The Department is responsible in part for the formulation of manpower and related policies, but primarily for their operation. As a relatively new Department with responsibilities for policies which involve the Department of Finance (and concern other older Departments), the Department of Labour is at a disadvantage in exercising influence on the development of policies for which it is operationally responsible.

2.4 While the Department of Labour is primarily responsible for Government policy in the areas of training, employment services, and industrial relations, it is not effectively involved in macro-economic forecasting or the budgetary decision-making process. One consequence is that the Department is responsible for manpower policies without participating in decisions which affect the economic environment in which those policies operate. Another is that decisions on the general "management" of the economy may be taken without sufficient information and advice on the implications for manpower and manpower policies.

2.5 The Irish economy has a history of high unemployment coupled more recently with rapid inflation and slow economic growth. As a result Irish manpower problems and policies concerned with them have come into greater prominence in recent years. Membership of the EEC, with the necessary economic adaptation, means that their importance may well increase.

2.6 We consider that manpower problems will need to be given fuller and more expert consideration in Irish policy-making. The way in which this can best be done is a matter for determination by the Irish Government. We consider, however, that the Department of Labour could make a more effective contribution in economic forecasting and budgetary decision-making and that its role in these matters might be formally recognised.

2.7 Participation by the Department in economic planning would increase the expertise of the planning group and extend the range of policies taken into account by those concerned with general economic policy. Greater use of active manpower policies in overall economic management would, we think, add to the effectiveness of other economic policies.

2.8 We give two examples: So far Irish policy has taken little account of the positive contribution which training can make to achieving short- and medium-term economic objectives; in addition, of course, to the longer term result of raising skill levels and thus real incomes. The employment service could also contribute to a more dynamic short-run manpower policy which could be particularly useful as the Irish economy readjusts following EEC membership.

2.9 The Department of Labour may not at present be adequately staffed and organised to perform the role we suggest in paragraphs 2.6 and 2.7. It has few staff qualified to interpret economic information, to contribute to the design of active manpower policies, to complement short-term economic strategy; or to forecast developments in the manpower field and examine policy options for possible application in the future. These functions might require the establishment of a specialised unit in the Department, staffed by professional economists, statisticians (and perhaps psychologists). Such a unit should develop contacts with professional work on manpower problems undertaken in the universities and professional institutes. This would have the secondary advantage of increasing the usefulness of such work for Government policy-making. The Devlin Report on the Organisation of the Public Service has recommended the addition of staff units in each Department to be concerned with planning, finance, organisation and personnel. We would positively recommend the adoption of this proposal.

2.10 In addition to the contribution which a specialist unit could make to the Department's changed role in relation to general economic strategy, it would provide valuable expertise for the Department's current policy responsibilities. Programme budgeting is becoming more important in the management and determination of Irish manpower policies. A specialised unit could provide advanced techniques of programme appraisal which would contribute to the development of a sound programme budgeting system.

2.11 We recommend the establishment of a specialist "research" unit in the Department of Labour to act as a focal point for the Department's contribution to formulation of macro-economic policy, be responsible for the evaluation of alternative manpower policies and to act as an advisory group on programme budgeting.

THE ROLE OF THE DEPARTMENT OF LABOUR IN REGIONAL POLICY

2.12 A positive regional policy centred around the industrial promotion activities of the Industrial Development Authority is the basis for the development of the Irish economy over the next twenty years. The objectives of the development policy are set out in the Government's statement of May 1972, and the policy is based on the belief that the key to economic expansion is the attraction of internationally mobile industry. The characteristics of the Irish economy lend support to a policy of encouraging additional industrial investment, although we have queried the suitability of highly selective incentives for this purpose.

2.13 In 1971, 26.3% of the Irish work force were employed in agriculture, a figure exceeded by only four other OECD countries. The agricultural population fell at an average rate of 10,000 per year over the period 1961–1971 although this rate of decline is expected to slow down following membership of the EEC which will result in an improvement in the price of agricultural products and home farm incomes. However, the numbers engaged in agriculture will continue to fall. Existing domestically-owned industry is concentrated in industries such as clothing and food processing, which have relatively modest growth prospects. There were over 70,000 (6.3%) unemployed in September 1972. It is evident that the expansion in employment opportunities required implies extensive new industrial investment, much of which must originate abroad.

2.14 The immediate objective of the Industrial Development Authority (and SFADCO in the mid-west region) is to attract more industry to Ireland. But the purpose of this is to create employment. While the IDA and SFADCO rightly have a major role in the formulation and execution of regional policy, it is essential that the real purpose – more jobs – is given appropriate weight in this policy. The views of the manpower authorities should be heard at the top level of the leading regional development bodies, particularly as effective manpower policies on such matters as training and placement are essential to success.

2.15 The Department of Labour is not represented on the boards of either the IDA or SFADCO. The basic responsibility for determining the levels of assistance offered to potential investors is exercised at board level in the two organisations. It is here that the manpower implications of each potential development should be given full consideration, and it seems to us that the Department of Labour needs to be represented. As a basic step towards the efficient realisation of manpower objectives by regional industrial development we recommend that a senior official of the Department of Labour should be invited to join the boards of the IDA and SFADCO and to participate actively in the consideration of investment incentives.

III

THE ADMINISTRATION OF REGIONAL POLICY

3.1 The Government of the day set out the overall strategy for Irish regional development in a policy statement of May 1972. Overall employment targets, including a target for industrial employment expansion, for the period up to 1977 were also published in the January 1972 White Paper on EEC membership.

3.2 The regional breakdown of the industrial employment target was examined by the Industrial Development Authority in consultation with all interested bodies and Departments and was settled by the Government on the recommendation of the IDA. In their summary of the 1972 regional industrial plans the IDA state:

> " Our plans set a gross target of 55,000 new manufacturing jobs in the five years 1973–77. "
>
> " ...We realise that by publishing these plans we are saying in effect that, during the next five years, our success or failure can be judged not only against the target of 55,000 new jobs in manufacturing industry, but also by the regional distributions we propose. We believe the task can be accomplished by co-operative effort and on the assumptions set out in the plans "*.

3.3 This passage indicates that the IDA has accepted responsibility for planning the expansion of employment in manufacturing industry and the proposed regional distribution of such expansion. In the report the IDA also set out the requirements on Government Departments and other agencies for action in support of this programme by the provision of infrastructure, manpower, training requirements etc. The IDA, however, has no power to co-ordinate the activities of the Departments and agencies responsible for the provision of these essential supporting measures to the programme. The Department of Finance has attempted to take up this co-ordinating role, but the instructions to Departments have not gone beyond a requirement to take account of the Government statement of May 1972 in Allocating Resources and Planning their programmes.

3.4 We think it might be of interest to set down several questions about these administrative arrangements. Is it appropriate for an agency outside Government to be in effect responsible for establishing the objectives for

* "*Jobs to the People*", P.2 IDA Ireland 1972.

the expansion of employment in manufacturing industry and for regional development, or should responsibility be seen to be a Government concern and more firmly located within the system that determines overall economic strategy? Since policies for regional development and general economic growth are closely related, should not the responsibility for determining the objectives and managing the programmes for both policies be within the Government? Is there not a danger that a division of responsibility between the two policies will weaken Government commitment to a regional strategy and threaten its success?

3.5 We recognise that the operation of a state agency outside the normal government machine may be more flexible and free from inappropriate civil service practices and procedures. These advantages, however, apply to the detailed operation of policy, rather than the determination of employment objectives and their regional distribution. A more appropriate relationship between the IDA and Government objectives in consultation with the operational agencies and the agencies were given responsibility for achieving those objectives which are directly related to their operational functions.

3.6 The need for greater central Government participation in regional planning is reinforced by the problems of co-ordinating the provision of necessary services in each local area. The IDA has its own regional organisation which is responsible for the execution of the industrial development programme, but can only indicate need for the provision of roads, land, water, sewerage, power, transport and manpower. It does not have the power to co-ordinate these operations, though they are nevertheless essential to the achievement of its own objectives. A Regional Development Committee in the Department of local Government is responsible for co-ordination, but its powers appear to be inadequate for the purpose of achieving co-ordinated provision of service facilities. Regional Development Organisations representing local authorities and interests have been established in the planning regions, but they are purely advisory bodies and have no executive responsibilities. There is a comprehensive system of physical planning based on the local Government (Planning and Development) Act 1963 which gives substantial power and responsibilities to elected local authorities, but the authorities are not responsible to the Regional Development Organisations for the exercise of these powers.

3.7 Some features of current Irish regional policy may flow from this organisational structure. For example, there are no plans for the expansion of service industries as distinct from manufacturing as a component in regional development. The IDA might argue that the location of service industry is a function of industrial location and hence cannot form a dynamic element in regional development.

3.8 An attempt at co-ordinated central development planning of a type which might be appropriate for the whole country has been made in the Gaeltacht or native Irish-speaking areas of Ireland which present special regional development problems. The Gaeltacht development plans make specific reference to the contribution which service industries can make to regional development and set out to encourage service industries in areas which are geographically and socially rather less suited to service industry location than many of the IDA regions. The concentration of the IDA on the encouragement of the development of manufacturing industry may provide too narrow a base for the most powerful and influential regional development body to develop sound regional development strategy.

3.9 The co-ordination of the various elements necessary for regional development was cited by the IDA as one of the problems which has hindered regional development to date, and as the scale of development objectives is increased the problem will become more serious. The IDA cited the availability of local services as a common problem in local industrial development and the training and manpower authorities indicated the difficulties that face them as a result of not being involved in IDA forward thinking or current negotiations.

3.10 The development organisation whose operations most impressed us was the Shannon Free Airport Development Company, which was established originally as an organisation to develop the facility of the Shannon duty-free airport, but which has since extended its operations to assist industrial and service developments in the whole mid-west region. SFADCO has drawn up its own development plan for the mid-west region in which it operates as an agent for the IDA. The plan is consistent with overall IDA objectives, but is a more detailed attempt to identify requirements and allocate responsibilities for the provision of infrastructure, trained manpower and local facilities than the IDA regional plans. SFADCO set out clearly what specific action is required of local authorities and state operations in their area. Its executive power outside the airport complex is limited, but within its area of responsibility it has initiated training schemes, organised the provision of transportation and actively undertaken investment which is geared towards the achievement of local employment objectives. The achievements of SFADCO illustrate the advantages of a regional planning organisation based on a strong central unit co-ordinating and managing related local programmes.

3.11 The central Government regional planning effort adopts, in contrast to SFADCO, a programme-oriented approach, with powerful operational agencies responsible for programmes on a national basis. For this type of organisation to work effectively these separate programme activities need to be co-ordinated at a *national* level to ensure that the different operations are consistent with each other and the central objectives of the plan; and at a *local* level to ensure that all phases of planned developments take place efficiently. The creation of a strong central regional planning unit appears to be an essential prerequisite for a successful programme-oriented regional policy. This would, of course, remove the prime responsibility for determining and achieving the employment objectives of regional policy from the IDA. But it would avoid the possibility of an unbalanced approach to regional growth which tends to result from the central role being occupied by a development agency concerned with manufacturing industry and, most important, secure the effective co-ordination of infrastructure and manpower programmes within a set of planning objectives.

3.12 The danger of centralising power for regional development in this way is that local interests and characteristics may be less well understood and local initiative and interest which are essential to long-term development of the less advanced regions may be blunted. Also as much of the responsibility for investment and the provision of services rests at the local level, this responsibility cannot be effectively managed by a central controlling unit. These are serious disadvantages which might be met by the establishment of a regional planning authority in the nine planning regions or the granting of equivalent powers to the existing RDO's. The Regional planning authorities would have responsibility for the execution of all the strands of the development programme within their areas. Their efforts could be co-ordinated and controlled by the central control unit which would devise a target programme and budget in consultation with the regional authorities which combined to achieve the required national objectives. The current Regional Development Organisations shadow this role to some extent, but they lack executive responsibility, control and the effectiveness and positive approach which greater power at the regional level would bring forth. The SFADCO organisation has some features of a working model of the type of organisation which appears to work effectively in the Irish economic environment. It is in touch with local conditions and requirements, able to co-ordinate the different strands of local development and willing to take initiatives to achieve the results it requires.

3.13 Various additional elements could be added to the regional development programme if a strong central and regional organisation were created. A growth centre approach which offers the best opportunity of successful regional development would be more acceptable and more efficiently planned if the initiative behind the proposal was regional rather than central. SFADCO is essentially an example of a successful growth centre approach which has produced an efficient development core at Shannon/Limerick which has improved employment opportunities and social facilities for the population in the associated region. A much greater local commitment to plan objectives could be encouraged by a regional organisation which would be in a position to take positive steps, such as the creation of facilities in advance of demand, if realisation threatened to fall short of objectives. At the moment it is difficult to see how local initiative can be harnessed or how central policies can be translated efficiently into action at the regional level. We think that re-organisation along these lines should be considered seriously since it would increase the effectiveness of the Irish regional planning effort.

IV

THE EMPLOYMENT SERVICE

THE ESTABLISHMENT OF THE NATIONAL MANPOWER SERVICE

4.1 Market information is a basic requirement of any resource allocation system. The justification for the provision of centralised market information in the labour market is that the individual search or marketing process is imperfect and very time consuming. Hence it may be more efficient to provide a centralised system which can offer considerable returns to scale. In principle it is possible to evaluate a manpower service in terms of benefits and costs. The benefits will be both social and economic, primarily in terms of search time saved for the customers and more efficient placement of job seekers, and the costs will mainly consist of the costs of the administrative framework.

4.2 The Irish placement service had developed as part of the social welfare administration with a large number of local offices concerned with the compilation of the live register of unemployment, the payment of state social welfare benefits to those on the register who were eligible for them, and the provision of assistance to the unemployed to obtain fresh employment. Priority was given to the payment of benefits so that the administrative functions of registration and payment dominated the work of the local employment exchanges. Placement and vocational guidance were given lower priority. Moreover, the fact that the offices combined the payment and placement functions made them less able to attract customers or the most suitable type of staff.

4.3 The Irish Government has recognised that the joint operation of the benefit payment and placement functions prevents the employment exchanges from playing an effective role in career guidance and placement. A team of consultants was appointed to examine the operation of the employment exchange system in 1966, and following from their recommendations and further consideration the new National Manpower Service was established. Under the new system the original employment exchanges will retain their benefit payment functions and will be controlled by the Department of Social Welfare, and the NMS will be located in separate premises more suitable for a placement and guidance service. The National Manpower Service became fully operational in September, 1971. It is thus a new and growing service and it is difficult to judge its performance over so short a time. It may however be appropriate to give our views as to how the service should be developed over the next few years.

THE ROLE OF THE NATIONAL MANPOWER SERVICE

4.4 The NMS has four basic functions. It is responsible for:

(*1*) Placing the unemployed in employment and meeting employer demands for labour of all types.

(*2*) The provision of regular information on the numbers and characteristics of the unemployed to the central statistics office for the purpose of compiling the Live Register.

(*3*) The provision of vocational guidance on employment training and educational opportunities for adult workers.

(*4*) The provision of careers information material to schools.

The responsibilities of the NMS are broadly in line with the recommendations of the consultants report, and we consider them appropriate. There are two matters only on which we wish to comment. First, advice and placement at the school leaver age and secondly vocational guidance for adults.

4.5 It is possible to identify two distinct guidance requirements of the school child to help him or her make a decision about a future career and to make a successful start in that career. Firstly, the child requires a wide ranging education about life beyond the school leaving age and the major part which employment will play in this life. This will be a preparation for choosing and making a success of a career. Secondly, at the time of leaving school and entering the labour market, the child will need more specific guidance as to the mechanics of getting a job and the specific employment opportunities available.

4.6 This distinction between forms of advice implies a distinction between the functions and requirements of a suitable adviser. The first function is primarily of an educational character, involving a wide ranging approach to the provision of information on alternative activities during the working years. The effectiveness of this educational stage will be greatly enhanced by an understanding of the attributes and personality of the child in question, and it will be more effective if undertaken on a relatively informal basis by someone with whom the child can feel confident to discuss personal plans.

4.7 The nature of this educational function strongly suggests that this role should be, as it is now, undertaken by specialised vocational guidance instructors in the schools. Vocational guidance teachers, specialising in this function, are already available in many large schools. Each teacher receives a one year full-time training course in vocational and educational guidance counselling and, in addition, teachers attend local seminars and short summer courses. Since September 1972, all guidance teachers in schools with over 250 pupils have been excluded from the teaching quota and are available for guidance work full-time. We are convinced that the education system has a major role to play in counselling the young and that this function merits the provision of full-time trained staff. We support the Irish Government's efforts to see that such a service is made available to all school children.

4.8 The function of actually placing a school-leaver in a job for the first time seems to involve rather different requirements of the responsible adviser. Ideally the adviser should have had first-hand experience of an industrial and commercial environment so as to be able to guide the applicant into a function and environment which will best suit his personality and requirements. The adviser must also be well acquainted with local and national job opportunities, which requires access to and the ability to interpret information on labour demand and supply. These requirements seem to be more closely related to the experience and characteristic of the local placement officer than to the guidance teacher. We would therefore recommend that consideration should be given to the possibility of entrusting to the NMS the responsibility for the placement of school leavers in employment.

4.9 The distinction between the functions of the school guidance officers and the placement officer will clearly not be a very precise one. It is to be expected that the school guidance function would be undertaken with the assistance of the placement officer, particularly in the provision of careers information material and preliminary discussion of employment opportunities. In addition the school guidance officer will have an understanding of the personality and attributes of a particular child which would be of great assistance to the placement officer in carrying out his function. The existence of some flexibility in the system would be particularly useful at a time when the NMS is still in the process of building up its facilities and service. As the education system already has vast experience of performing this guidance function and there are perhaps more pressing problems of adult unemployment before the manpower service, it would perhaps be wise to refrain from a major expansion of NMS first placement functions until the current objectives for the scale of the manpower service have been achieved.

4.10 The general operation of the National Manpower Service would be improved over time by its having responsibility for the placement of school leavers and this would benefit both the service and its customers. Young people would identify the NMS as the provider of information and advice on employment matters and would turn to the service for such assistance much more readily at a later stage. If the objective of the service is to meet the requirements of all employees or potential employees for advice and information on employment matters, responsibility for the first job placing would seem an integral part of the function of the National Manpower Service.

4.11 A related activity to guidance for school leavers is vocational guidance for adults. This is explicitly recognised as a basic objective of the National Manpower Service, but the training and work of the placement officers are not yet fully geared to the provision of this service, and no full-time vocational guidance officers have been appointed to the service. In the first few years of its operation, the NMS has been concentrating on placement work rather than the provision of vocational guidance. This is understandable, but while filling the biggest possible number of job vacancies is most important the basic objective of matching labour supply with labour demand implies more than placing x men in x jobs. The quality of each placement is also very important and should be given a high priority, even in the early stages of the operation of the NMS. We feel that the service should not allow placement to overlay its guidance role, and recommend that more thought should be given to the provision of vocational guidance services.

4.12 There is an element of vocational guidance work in each placement that the NMS will be called on to perform, and it is therefore necessary that each placement officer should receive a basic training in guidance techniques. In some cases fairly fundamental guidance problems will present themselves, and the skill and experience of the placement officers who will not be primarily concerned with this function will be inadequate to meet the requirements of these cases. We therefore think that the NMS will require to appoint and train specialist guidance officers to work alongside the placement officers. In view of the importance of building a good reputation in the early years of the NMS and the integral nature of guidance in the work of the service, it is advisable that the need to provide specialist vocational guidance should be recognised and met promptly. We would recommend that consideration should be given to the initiation of a recruitment and training programme to provide a basic cadre of vocational guidance officers in the NMS within the next two to three years.

4.13 Our recommendations for the development of a comprehensive first placement and increased attention to vocational guidance for adult workers have implications for both the scale of the NMS and the training of its staff. We deal with these in paragraphs 4.21–4.27.

4.14 The adequacy of current training provisions for placement officers can only be assessed in the light of their job experiences, and it is not possible for us to indicate precise improvements in current training. Vocational guidance however, is one subject in which placement officers will not have had experience in their previous jobs, and this is one area where training provisions need to be improved. The experience of the Department of Education in training career guidance teachers provides a source of expertise and a systematic series of lectures, case studies and discussions of guidance techniques might be usefully fitted into the training of placement officers. A course of this nature could be designed to meet the requirements of both the vocational guidance and first placement functions of the placement officers.

ADMINISTRATION OF THE NATIONAL MANPOWER SERVICE

4.15 A key issue in the establishment of a placement service is the relationship of the service to the administration of manpower policy. The National Manpower Service has been set up as an operational division of the Department of Labour, staffed very largely by persons recruited from the industrial and business world and trade unions. The Service is bound by Civil Services rules on financial control, terms and conditions of appointment and recruitment procedure. This is a logical step because the service has grown up from the employment exchange system which has been and will remain in the Civil Service and the operations of the NMS related to manpower policies which are the concern of the Department of Labour.

4.16 There are, however, operational disadvantages. Each major item of expenditure which the NMS wishes to undertake – such as the acquisition of new premises – has to be approved by the sponsoring Department and the Department of Finance, so that decisions which involve expenditure are not easy. As all the members of the staff on appointment become civil servants, they are recruited by the Civil Service Commission and paid a salary determined by civil service relativities.

4.17 We have the impression that these arrangements have imposed restrictions on the building up of the service, the numbers of high quality staff who have applied for posts and the style of operation of the service. Quicker progress should be possible if the service was under less detailed restraint in obtaining premises and staff and had more freedom to take decisions in these respects which influence its performance and style. This could we think be combined with the necessary degree of general control over costs. The success of the service in establishing a reputation as an effective provider of job information, guidance and labour will be greatly influenced by its performance in the early years of its existence. The service would benefit by being seen to be more a part of the up-to-date commercial life of Ireland than a more traditional Civil Service operation.

4.18 In the report of the Devlin Committee on the organisation of the Irish Civil Service, particular attention was paid to the methods of efficiently carrying out executive as distinct from policy-making functions. The Devlin recommendation, based on this distinction, was that policy-making should be entrusted to the central core of each Government Department, grouped around the Minister, and the execution of specific responsibilities should be entrusted to satellite bodies reporting to the central core. These bodies would differ in nature from the Irish concept of the semi-state agency in that they would still be responsible to a particular Department rather than a Governing board representative of the bodies concerned with the work of the agency. The advantages of a Devlin type executive agency are that its objectives and policy would remain the responsibility of the parent Department, while the agency would be responsible for its own administrative decisions and executive activity with freedom of executive action within a central budget.

4.19 This type of administrative set-up would appear to meet the principal objective of operating the NMS within the Government by making it clearly responsible to the manpower policy-making department. At the same time the NMS could have freedom of action in its day to day affairs within a general budget constraint. The operational success of the NMS could then be assessed in the light of the efficiency with which it achieved its objectives within its budget. We see considerable advantage in this type of administrative set-up for the operation of executive functions of the type for which the National Manpower Service is responsible, and recommend that the possibility of establishing the National Manpower Service as an executive agency should be seriously considered.

4.20 One other vital element in the early years of the National Manpower Service is support from employers and worker organisations. These bodies have contacts with a large number of potential NMS customers and their support and involvement in the building up of the NMS may be critical to its success. The establishment of the NMS as an executive agency one step removed from the Department of Labour could help to persuade employer and worker organisations that they have a responsibility for and would benefit from participating actively in the development of the NMS.

4.21 More needs to be done to increase contact between the NMS and its actual potential customers at the top decision-making level. A valuable attribute of the Irish semi-state agency form of organisation is that a wide range of opinion is represented at the higher levels, which produces a sense of involvement from those bodies concerned with a particular activity. The current organisation of the NMS does not provide the opportunity to involve employer or worker organisations in an advisory or decision taking role, and it might be useful to move towards this by setting up a multipartite body at the head of the NMS consisting of the Director and leading figures in Irish industry and trade unions. In order to generate a spirit of commitment amongst the union and management participants, it might be advisable to grant the body broad executive powers in the field of planning and budgetary control. Such a development would then encourage the employers and workers to adopt a more positive attitude vis-à-vis the service. Such a body could easily be fitted into an executive agency structure.

THE OPERATION OF THE NATIONAL MANPOWER SERVICE

4.22 Having dealt with basic policy issues of the function and organisation of the NMS we comment briefly on its operational practices and staffing and recommend possible improvements.

4.23 The current objective of the service is to achieve a cadre of some 220 staff, 90 of whom would be placement officers, by the end of 1976. The staff is to be distributed amongst 8 regional and 22 local offices. We consider that the geographical dispersion of the service is adequate for Irish needs. Efficiency argues against having a larger number of permanent offices in every town staffed by only one or two placement officers. The dispersion of 22 local offices should enable the staff to keep in close touch with the employment situation in surrounding towns and villages, and no centres of population will be outside easy travelling distance from one or more local offices. Providing a service to job seekers in the more isolated locations may require more positive steps to establish contact with each local community, and for this it may be useful if temporary accommodation could be provided at which the placement officer could be present at regular intervals. This facility should improve the penetration of the service in the more remote areas.

4.24 Since the service became operational in September 1971, it has built up a staff of 6 Regional Directors and 24 Placement Officers in a period of twelve months. This is a fairly rapid rate of expansion, based on the belief that a comprehensive national service should be available by the end of 1975.

4.25 As we have said we do not think this scale of operation will be adequate to perform the full range of tasks appropriate to the NMS. In view of the current difficulty the NMS is experiencing in providing adult vocational guidance on a sufficiently comprehensive basis and in the light of our recommendation to extend its operations into first placement of school leavers, the present target of 90 placement staff seems inadequate. It is difficult to suggest a precise alternative figure, but our recommendations imply at least a 50% increase in the number of expert staff. Rather than set an arbitrary staff target or ceiling at this stage it might be better that placement officers should assess the staffing implications of meeting the demands for placement, vocational guidance and career planning in their own areas as their functions develop and feed this information up to the central management unit which could then determine the correct scale of the total NMS operation. A suitably revised target rate of expansion might aim at achieving a staffing level of 135 placement officers (approximately 150% of the current target of 90) by the end of 1976.

4.26 The NMS are expanding as rapidly as possible within the existing recruitment constraints. If these constraints could be weakened or removed, we believe that the target we have suggested should be attainable. Some of the present difficulties of expansion are due to administrative problems which an executive-agency structure would help to alleviate. As experience in the recruitment and training of staff is gained, more office facilities will become available and the longer serving staff will become more experienced and effective. The NMS should be in a position to maintain a rate of expansion at least as rapid as it has achieved to date, and this should be sufficient to achieve the revised staffing target by 1976.

4.27 The basic thinking behind our recommendations for changes in the administration of the NMS has been the desire to establish it as a highly effective service within the Irish economic system, guiding manpower to the most rewarding and most suitable activities. A number of specific possibilities to this end were discussed during our meetings with the Irish authorities, and it might be useful if we were to set out our response to some of these.

4.28 One possibility was that use of the service might be made compulsory. There are a number of alternatives. For example, all public bodies could be required to recruit exclusively through the NMS or all employers could be required to notify vacancies to the service. While the service is still in the process of building up from a small base, the proposal that it should handle all public sector recruitment would not fit in with the relatively small scale of its operation and the desire that it should be actively involved in private sector placements of all types of employee. A concentration on public sector placement which would probably have to be restricted to lower grade appointments in view of the established role of the Civil Service Commission, would not provide either the experience or the image which the service requires. We therefore think that compulsory use of the NMS by public bodies would not be useful.

4.29 The possibility of compulsory vacancy notification has rather more attractions. At present, Irish firms give little or no notice of likely increases in demand for workers, and the existing NMS offices have only a sketchy knowledge of the vacancy situations in their area. The more comprehensive the vacancy information the NMS can obtain the more rapidly and successfully it will be able to undertake its tasks of placing and redirecting labour. The provision of vacancy information is not an onerous task, and in a high unemployment economy with consequent high social value from additional employment, there is a good case for requiring the most comprehensive information on labour demand which can be readily made available. In the light of the employment situation and the value of information about jobs to the NMS we believe there is a good case for requiring all public sector employers to make a regular return of vacancies to the NMS. All private sector firms above a certain size (say 5 to 10 employees) would be encouraged to follow suit. Each employer would be given a simple form, which he could complete perhaps weekly, which would summarise his current and projected labour requirements. This information would be gathered and processed by the regional NMS offices and presented in the form of both local, regional and national employment opportunity lists to the various NMS offices. The information would also be useful to bodies other than the NMS, particularly the regional development teams and AnCO. It could be fed into the regional planning authorities as a valuable adjunct to their information on current and future employment conditions. A similar policy of compulsory redundancy notification in the public sector and improved incentives to the private sector might also bring considerable benefit.

4.30 A second issue which was raised in our discussions with the Irish authorities was that of publicising the new National Manpower Service. The dissemination of information on the role of the service and the financial and advisory services which it can offer is vital to its success, and the publicity so far accorded the service has been inadequate for the purpose of bringing its existence to the attention of the population as a whole. The NMS argue that too much publicity for the service when it is still in its infancy could attract a larger number of people than the service could handle efficiently. The reputation of the service would then suffer and it might never get off the ground at all. We sympathise with this view, but believe that the NMS is in danger of overrating the danger and underrating the value of publicity in the early years. Our recommendation that a top level management body representing employer and worker organisations should be formed to assist in the development of the NMS, should open fresh channels of communication. The granting of executive agency status would also give the body more freedom of action which we trust would encourage a more positive marketing policy. One potentially useful development which we witnessed was the use by the NMS of the medium of the press for advertising specific employment vacancies. This is a welcome indication of the positive role in Irish manpower policy which the NMS is adopting. The willingness of private employment agencies to advertise specific positions and thus indirectly their own organisations seems to have been a significant factor in their growth in Ireland and the United Kingdom. We do not feel that this method of operation is inappropriate for a public body such as the NMS, and think there is a good case for its going further. Advertising will be particularly appropriate for the higher skilled jobs where the supply of potential employees tends to be limited. If in undertaking positive marketing of its services the NMS becomes involved in advice to the employed rather than placement of the unemployed, we would not consider this a matter for serious concern. The service has an important role to play in guiding labour effectively, and in doing so it will continuously create fresh employment opportunities which ultimately will benefit the unemployed.

THE FINANCE OF THE NATIONAL MANPOWER SERVICE

4.31 The extent to which the State should carry financial responsibility for the provision of training and employment services is a problem which concerns all of the OECD Member Governments. The cost of State finance for training, education and employment services is increasing rapidly in Ireland, though it is not as yet at a relatively high per capita level. Several features of the Irish situation justify the increase. Many of the services are relatively new and still developing. Government initiative has been necessary to initiate and speed up development and until the benefits of these services become more widely appreciated, continuing State support will be necessary. The extent of unemployment is a powerful argument in favour of an active public expenditure policy, as successful policy will have a high benefit/cost pay-off.

4.32 In our analysis of Irish policies for industrial training we have concluded however that the State should not continue to be primarily responsible for providing industrial training and that the responsibility should in time pass largely to employers who benefit from it. We consider that the same principle might to some extent apply in the longer run to some of the employment service, although the role of the State as the operator of the employment service must clearly be maintained.

4.33 The re-organisation of the NMS as an executive agency would make possible a more flexible financial policy. While the service is building up its capacity, experience and reputation, we consider that the whole cost should be met from public funds. Even in the longer term many of its operations will have a social value exceeding the subjective private valuation and the willingness of the private individual or organisation to meet the cost. It is right that the State should continue to finance activities of this nature as carried out by the employment service. Certain specialist functions of the service may not fall within this criterion. The provision of job information and the recruitment of highly qualified employees are examples where employers may well value the assistance of the NMS above the marginal cost of the service provided. In such cases where the market will bear all or a substantial part of the cost of providing a service, we suggest that the employment service might sometime in the future give thought to the provision of specialist services, say for the recruitment of executive personnel, and charge for the provision of the service.

V

MANPOWER INFORMATION

THE NEED FOR MANPOWER INFORMATION

5.1 Information on current and future manpower requirements, the current and future supply of manpower and the characteristics of the labour market are needed for purposes of developing manpower policies to assist the achievement of general economic objectives.

5.2 The problem of deciding how much information to collect is difficult in practice as the benefits of additional manpower information are sometimes indirect and difficult to quantify. We first review the extent to which current Irish manpower information meets the policy-making requirements felt by the manpower authorities and those responsible for general economic policy.

INFORMATION CURRENTLY AVAILABLE

5.3 Information about the supply of manpower is currently provided by three main sources:

1. Population census;
2. Live Register;
3. Local labour surveys.

The census provides the most comprehensive set of information, providing data on the whole population classified by sex and age group, location, occupation, industry and employment status. The census is taken quinquennially and takes between one and three years to process and publish. Its coverage of the population is, for all practical purposes, complete. It provides comprehensive information but it only indicates long-term trends and is already out of date by the time it is published. More seriously, because of its periodicity, the census data are seriously out of date by the time a fresh census is performed. For example, insofar as age, industrial and occupational classifications are concerned, the Irish are currently operating on data from the April 1966 census – seven years old. In an economy experiencing significant structural changes and variations in substantial emigration movements the information is of limited value for manpower policy-making.

5.4 An attempt is made to interpolate some of the census statistics for inter-censal years by using survey information from the Annual Agricultural Enumeration and the Census of Industrial Production. This supplementary information is of limited use as it varies in its reliability and coverage and provides data only on particular sectors of the labour force.

5.5 The Live Register of Unemployed provides information on a weekly basis of the numbers registering for unemployment benefit and unemployment assistance and other persons registering for employment who are not claiming benefit. Information on numbers, sex and age (classified simply juveniles, adults and those over 65) is produced weekly, information on the age breakdown of males is produced monthly, industrial and occupational breakdowns quarterly and duration of unemployment annually.

5.6 The Live Register data have a number of significant shortcomings as a basic source of labour force information. As with all such registers, no information is obtained of people who might be willing to work if a suitable job was available but who are ineligible or do not take the trouble to register for benefit. School leavers are not eligible for unemployment benefit, so there is also little incentive for them to register. Non-manual employees earning over £1,600 per annum and the self-employed are excluded from the social security system and very few therefore register.

5.7 Local labour market surveys have been undertaken in a number of small towns earmarked for potential industrial development. These have produced detailed information on the unemployed, potential employees, school leavers and local labour demand which has been of use to the development planners. The information is not comprehensive on an overall or national basis as the surveys have been undertaken only on a one – off basis in about 15 scattered localities around the country.

5.8 Labour demand information is much scarcer, although the absence of adequate information of this type is typical of more advanced economies than the Irish. A policy of small scale local development planning which is currently in operation in Ireland, requires fairly comprehensive local labour demand information for it to be effective, and the information currently available in Ireland is inadequate. No data are gathered on a systematic basis. Broad employment trends by industry are estimated by the Department of Industry and Commerce through the industrial review system. The IDA gather some information of varying reliability about the employment opportunities of new investments which they support, and the local labour market surveys gather information on identifiable future labour demands from employers in the study area. The sum of this information does not provide an overall or detailed labour demand and supply picture.

ADDITIONAL INFORMATION REQUIREMENTS

5.9 In view of the severe manpower problems which are facing the Irish Government, the detailed regional development strategy which is being followed, and the importance which manpower issues and policies will assume with membership of the EEC, we consider that the presently available manpower data are inadequate for manpower policy design and control. We think it might be useful to give some indication of the principal gaps in current statistics.

(*1*) The first weakness of current manpower information is that it seriously understates the available labour supply in Ireland. This situation may account in part for the inability of Irish economic policies to alleviate the problem of chronic unemployment through aiming at too low an expansion rate. Now that Ireland is in the EEC, structural change in the Irish economy is expected to accelerate and economic policy will need to be more radical for Ireland to compete effectively. More active policy will require a more comprehensive study of the labour supply situation. Four groups of actual or potential employees on whom labour supply information is currently inadequate can be identified. Non-manual employees and school leavers are inadequately represented in the live register, married women have a limited economic and social incentive to register for employment, and a large number of workers, primarily in the agricultural sector, are underemployed and thus not contributing as effectively as they might to income creation. More information on these groups would mobilise and guide policy to make improved use of the country's labour resources.

(*2*) Current information is also inadequate on the individual characteristics of the actual or potential labour supply. Information on the skill and occupational characteristics of the unemployed, their age and the extent of long-term unemployment is required for both local and national manpower policy. The provision of this information is infrequent and imprecise.

(*3*) An outstanding characteristic of the Irish labour market is the extent of labour migration to the United Kingdom and the relative unwillingness of the adult labour force to migrate internally. The flow of Irish emigrants is concentrated in the employable age groups and probably includes a large number of trained individuals whose productive potential is lost to the Irish economy. The flow is large and variable, apparently dependant largely on economic conditions in Ireland and the United Kingdom. For Irish macro-economic policy to be successful in terms of maximising domestic expansion, account needs to be taken of migratory movements, and this requires information on their cause and extent. Policies for the development of education, training and job opportunities need to take account of the migration problem, and might attempt to minimise both the outflow of trained labour and the impact of the outflow on the domestic balance between labour demand and supply. Policies to improve the mobility of labour within the country also require information on migratory behaviour.

(*4*) Information on a regional and local level is also inadequate. Labour demand information at this level is critical to the success of the Irish regional strategy. The provision of educational and training facilities, investment in local services and infrastructure and the scale and nature of local manpower services should all take account of future demand developments. Local development assistance should be undertaken in the light of information on the forecast demands of existing activity and local labour supply characteristics. Without such information the various economic policies cannot be assured of achieving specific manpower policy objectives.

METHODS OF OBTAINING ADDITIONAL INFORMATION

5.10 The most obvious method of improving the data currently available would be to gather more information from existing data sources. The value of Census of Population data is severely circumscribed by the periodicity of the census and the lag involved in processing the information. The addition of more information to the census would make the tasks of administering and participating in the census more onerous and the analysis of results might be even further delayed. Performing a complete census more frequently would be a very costly way of gathering that part of the census information which is required more frequently. Neither of these courses of action promise to produce the type of information required in an efficient manner, and we would not recommend a modification of the existing census system as a means of gathering more manpower information.

5.11 The fact that the live register is a by-product of the social security system, which is based on different objectives from those of manpower policy, restricts the opportunity of improving the usefulness of this source of information. Some improvement in the periodicity with which age, skill, occupation and unemployment duration characteristics are published might be possible, but would only partially meet the requirements of the manpower policy makers. It is basically inappropriate that vital manpower information should be a by-product of a service which is designed to meet quite different objectives, and we would thus not recommend an attempt to build the live register into the basic source of manpower information.

5.12 The local labour market surveys can provide detailed information of a type which is really useful for guiding investment assistance and indicating the characteristics of the labour supply of a particular area. A series of these *ad hoc* local surveys undertaken by study teams which are unfamiliar with the locality in question would not meet the periodicity and cost effectiveness requirements of a comprehensive manpower information system however, and we do not consider that this approach could provide the basic information required by the manpower policy makers.

5.13 Our conclusion is that all the present sources are inadequate for the purpose of providing the type of manpower information which is necessary for manpower planning and that none of these sources provides a satisfactory framework on which a comprehensive information system could be established.

5.14 In view of the varied characteristics of the problems on which information is required it does not appear that any single system would meet all the requirements of the manpower authorities. We make a number of suggestions about how the present system might be improved, which we hope will be useful.

5.15 We do not feel that the Census of Population is a particularly suitable vehicle for obtaining manpower information and think that a periodic national labour market survey, undertaken annually or biennially, on a sample basis would be more useful. A statistically significant sample of the population could be covered at relatively modest cost, and a reduction in the scale of the Census of Population which would result would meet at least part of the cost of the labour market surveys. The information gathered by this means could be adapted to the requirements of the manpower authorities and, in view of the relatively small number of returns, processed more rapidly than the Census of Population data. On balance this source of manpower information would appear to be the most cost effective method of obtaining basic labour market data.

5.16 A sample labour market survey on a national basis would not provide all the detailed local information on labour supply and demand necessary for implementation of development objectives at the regional and local level. This information might be collected through local manpower offices. The National Manpower Service is the greatest potential beneficiary of such information, and some part of the placement officers' time is already spent on gathering local labour market information. If the role of the National Manpower Service in providing such manpower information were systematised and resources specifically allocated for this purpose, an efficient data collection system could be developed. This type of detailed information on unemployment, school leavers, potential employees and identifiable labour demand is most useful if it is obtained systematically and reliably. It might be helpful to nominate an officer (possibly full-time) in each NMS regional office whose job it would be to supply comprehensive information on the regional labour market to the Regional Development Organisation and to the relevant central Government bodies. This form of organisation would fit naturally into the regional development structure and the information generated would considerably enhance the executive-type regional development programme which we have recommended.

5.17 Certain specific Irish manpower problems remain which are inadequately covered by a scheme of labour market surveys and regional information officers. The scale and nature of emigration; the problem and potential of the underemployed; and the possibility of developing advanced econometric forecasting techniques to a level at which they can contribute to the design of Government manpower policy are all subjects on which comprehensive research is required. The research unit which we have proposed should be established in the Department of Labour (Chapter 2), should have the technical capacity to undertake research of the type necessary to complement the regular channels of manpower information, and the potential value of research on these specific problems of manpower policy lends further support to our recommendation for the establishment of such a professional research unit in the Department of Labour.

VI

TRAINING AND EDUCATION

6.1 The team agree with the view put to them by the Irish authorities who say that:

> "it is expected that industrial training will continue to be the key element in manpower policy in the 1970s and problems arising under this heading will be a major preoccupation of the manpower authorities".

In view of our knowledge and experience we have concentrated this section of our analysis on skill training rather than educational facilities, whilst recognising that the two subjects are interdependent and often indistinguishable. We comment briefly on the post primary educational system and the relationship between education and the labour market at the end of this chapter.

6.2 In the next decade employment in Irish agriculture will continue to decline (see Chapter II); employment in existing service and industrial operations will expand and new industry will be attracted to Ireland. These changes are likely to be accelerated by membership of the European Economic Community. They will require a substantial and continuing effort to improve the numbers and quality of skilled manpower. A high priority for training and retraining is necessary for the economic changes which are an integral part of Irish growth strategy in the 1970s and beyond. If maximum expansion of the economy is to be achieved it is vital that skilled labour be available to meet the needs of expanding Irish industry and to complement the fiscal investment incentives being offered to attract new industry. Doubts about the availability of trained labour will hamper these developments and it is vital therefore that manpower policy and training in particular should be accorded its due role in the expansion programme.

6.3 The considerable geographical and occupational imbalances which characterise the Irish economy have been highlighted earlier in our report. Their existence suggests that there is great scope for increasing internal mobility between jobs and regions in Ireland. In a social cost-benefit analysis the benefits of a training programme are usually estimated by using the resultant increase in wages as a proxy for the increase in productivity. The costs are the institutional ones of providing the training facility and the opportunity costs for the persons undergoing training. For a person otherwise unemployed the second item will generally be nil.

6.4 Training does more than assist economic expansion by ensuring that sufficient workers of the required skills are available in the right places at the right time. It is also an investment in human capital, which has social as well as economic benefits. The potential output (and earning capacity) of the individual is increased by fresh skills and, if successfully used, these skills benefit society as a whole. Training is thus a major element in both economic and social progress, and we consider that it should be given a high priority in Irish policies for more rapid growth and the improvement of community welfare.

6.5 A co-ordinated approach to training is necessary between Government authorities, industry and the educational system. The aim should be to ensure that firms carry out training sufficient to meet their own future needs and recognise in addition the social benefit to be gained from increased training. Ideally the Government should concentrate on the provision of grant aid to training for new industry, modernisation of the apprenticeship system and encouraging training in firms and training institutions for particular skills in short supply. The extent to which this selective approach will be possible will depend on the reaction of industry to the fresh impetus which Government encouragement of training is providing.

TRAINING BY THE FIRM: THE LEVY GRANT SYSTEM

6.6 The largest part of the training effort is arranged by employers to meet their own immediate or foreseeable needs. This is right. By providing training the employer avoids unnecessarily high costs arising from poor performance, delays, breakdowns, high labour turnover. Training needs vary from firm to firm according to local circumstances and only individual employers are in a position to decide what these needs are. There is evidence, however, that the benefits of training were not widely recognised by employers before the introduction of the Industrial Training Act (1967). One of the main aims of policy should be to ensure that the generality of employers recognise the value of training and are stimulated to assess their training needs.

6.7 However, there are a number of factors which dissuade a private person or a firm from undertaking training which would be socially desirable. The individual may lack information about training opportunities and potential private returns, he will not be able to obtain a loan to meet his personal training costs and living expenses over the training period, and the credit market will not be in a position to offer loans with the necessary guarantees against the risk of possible failure. An employer paying the cost of training will run the risk of losing the productivity benefit of the training if the newly trained employee moves to another firm.

6.8 There are a number of ways in which the Government can attempt to overcome these problems:

(*1*) Provide loans with the necessary guarantees and thus overcome the weakness of the credit market. This approach may be combined with a system of individual "drawing rights" which guarantee each member of the community the opportunity to engage in a minimum period of training during his working life, and provide resources from a central fund to finance the training or retraining. To date few countries have adopted this approach on a large scale, but more are moving in this direction, particularly in respect of university training.

(*2*) An alternative method of overcoming the market weakness is to subsidise individual training by providing large scale public facilities at low or nil cost to the trainee. This type of scheme will offer strong incentives for training which will have to be controlled by a selection mechanism. An obvious drawback of the system is that the selected individuals obtain most of the benefits from the training (apart from those taxed away or represented by an excess of productivity gain over higher wage payment) but bear a small proportion of the costs. This type of scheme may thus have the effect of intensifying skewness in the income distribution.

(*3*) A third approach is to internalise the costs and benefits of training within a group of firms. A theoretically perfect system would involve the firm paying a fee for each employee, equal to the periodised training costs of that employee, to a central fund which would then pay for training across the economy regardless of whether it took place in an institution or in another firm. Free mobility is guaranteed and an optimal allocation of resources is achieved without violation of equity in the income distribution if equal training opportunity is offered to all employees.

6.9 The levy/grant system used in Ireland and administered by AnCO is a somewhat crude variant of the third scheme. Every firm in an industry pays a certain percentage of its wage bill in the form of a levy to AnCO and in return is guaranteed a grant if it fulfils certain conditions regarding training. As a general rule it is not possible for a firm to receive a training grant in excess of its levy contribution. This means that some of the potential economic virtues of the third approach are lost. There is no guarantee that training takes place in the firm with a comparative advantage for training, and there are few incentives for training giving broader skills or increased mobility. In addition the system is administratively burdensome with a large amount of negotiation between individual firms and AnCO. Supplementary to this scheme AnCO also runs a retraining programme of a more traditional type – the second approach – although on a small scale – 1,200 places by the end of 1972.

6.10 It may in time prove possible to reduce the scale and extent of the levy/grant system, but it is not practicable now to recommend any particular timescale for this nor whether at a later date the system should be dropped or used more selectively. Decisions on these matters will depend on the extent to which the need for effective training of workers is accepted by senior management in the larger firms and the extent to which AnCO's professional advisory staff establish a reputation for effective advice on training systems. Meanwhile we have several suggestions to offer for the development of the work of AnCO.

6.11 We believe that AnCO should develop an effective organisation for advice and consultancy, in addition to its management of the levy/grant scheme, since many managements are inexperienced in training. In administering training grants, AnCO staff should be able to advise firms on the types of training programme needed and how to establish such programmes. An active advisory service on training, in addition to the financial aid, should persuade firms of the value of the levy/grant system and of their own training efforts.

6.12 AnCO might also provide a competent "consultancy" operation to give advice and guidance to employers on the spot. The consultants should be able to evaluate the training requirements of a firm and advise on staffing, training standards and techniques and assist in the placement of staff in training centres and technical colleges. The quality of consultancy staff will be vital to success and the service should therefore be built up from a limited number of really good staff who command the respect of managements. The same quality of staffing is required in the management strata of AnCO itself for the agency to maintain and improve its standing with Irish industry.

6.13 The Irish Management Institute are already providing a service which has somewhat similar features, although primarily directed at management and organisational needs. The IMI's In-Company Management Development Unit provides a consultancy service aimed at improving companies' business and human resources development and this can include advice on the assessment of training needs and the design and implementation of a full training programme to meet that need. The service is now 5 years old and is well developed, but it is appropriate to raise the question of how AnCO and IMI can best co-operate to ensure that the best service in the area of training can be given to Irish industry. The need for such a service is common throughout Irish Industry, and the rather larger scale and more comprehensive coverage of AnCO's operations might ensure that the scheme reaches the maximum audience. There would also appear to be a close relationship between the financial and advisory work of AnCO and the IMI's training services which would mean that both would benefit from a closer working relationship. This possibility might usefully be given serious consideration.

6.14 The training needs of smaller firms, say those with between 10 and 50 employees, require special treatment. We consider there is a need to develop services tailored to them, since in the longer term they are likely to require continuing outside support in training matters, e.g. their needs often arise sporadically and for this and other reasons it may be difficult to persuade owner-managers to undertake training themselves in training techniques. The best course might be for AnCO to develop a consultancy branch specialising in small firms, together with the provision of specific courses for small-firm managers, for example, at weekends. The present basis of exemptions from levy/grant of small firms (those with an annual wage bill of £5,000 to £20,000 depending on industry) is too small and needs redefinition according to the circumstances in each industrial sector.

TRAINING AND RETRAINING SCHEMES FOR INDIVIDUALS

6.15 We believe there will be a need over the next decade for a significant increase in the facilities available for training and retraining individual workers. In addition to the unemployed and those in rural areas who wish to obtain industrial employment, there will be a general demand for more skilled workers as compared with the present situation. A high proportion of such training and retraining schemes should aim to produce a level of skills at least equal to that gained through apprenticeship and generally recognised as such. It is difficult to estimate now the precise demands of the labour market in the future, but to plan for an expansion from the present level of a throughput of 0.2% of the labour force annually by the Government training centres to a level of 0.5 to 1% in five years' time would seem reasonable.

6.16 In view of the economic background presented earlier, there seem a priori to be great social benefits to be reaped in Ireland from further increases in the training programme. In an economy where wage differentials between skilled and unskilled average about £10 per week and where six months' intensive training is required from a technical point of view to achieve an upgrading, the pay-off period from a skill training programme would be little more than one year. There is thus every reason for attempting to train workers of all age groups. We were concerned to discover that only 10% of trainees in Government Training Centres were over 35 years old, and thought there should be more emphasis on the training or retraining of adults in higher age groups. To make training more attractive to potential trainees we recommend that consideration should be given to paying trainees a proportion (say 60 or 80%) of the normal wage for the occupation for which they are being trained. At present trainees receive only slightly more than the Unemployment Benefit rate and this is unlikely to attract good quality trainees, particularly from the older age groups.

6.17 We were encouraged by reports of an arrangement reached in Cork where a new training centre was opened in 1972. Adult trainees are being trained to a fully skilled level in engineering and existing craftsmen in engineering are being trained to up-grade their skills. The trainees are being accepted by the unions as suitable for skilled jobs in the industry. Full provision should be made for places in centres for upgrading skills. These needs will not be confined to manufacturing industry and certainly not to semi-skilled or skilled manual jobs. Shortages of all technicians, skilled people in the service trades and adequately trained middle management are more likely to prove bottlenecks to economic expansion, and will require further expansion of technical colleges, agricultural institutes and the INI facilities.

6.18 We believe that it might well be practicable to foresee in more detail particular areas where a shortage of skilled workers is likely to hold up progress. The National Manpower Service is setting up an information system on a regional basis for job vacancies and employee availability. This should be helpful. In addition, it would seem desirable to establish some point in the manpower service which would concentrate on identifying particular areas where a substantial additional training effort ought to be mounted. An attempt to create a manpower forecasting machine to cover all occupations would probably be less useful than a limited exercise drawing on all the information which can be made available through the manpower services, through AnCO, through industrial associations and through contacts with individual firms. There should also be studies of information on training from European and other sources and, where necessary, research specific to the Irish situation carried out to provide information required for proper planning of training provisions. The central role in this task might usefully be undertaken by the planning unit which we have recommended should be created in the Department of Labour.

6.19 We welcome the expansion in a number of Regional Technical Colleges which provide general educational programmes leading to technician, higher technician and in some cases professional qualifications, but suggest that it would be desirable to provide a wider range of courses covering more specialist as well as general industrial training.

APPRENTICESHIP

6.20 A review of the Irish apprenticeship system is in progress. Traditional apprenticeship schemes are being modified and brought into line with present-day needs throughout Western Europe. We are convinced of the importance of systematic off-the-job training in the first period of an apprenticeship and that apprenticeships should be broadly based in the early stages while enabling the apprentices to specialise in particular skills later on. We are certain that the tendency towards a shorter apprenticeship period is essential in present-day conditions. We hope that the changes in the apprenticeship system will be along these lines.

6.21 Apprenticeship of young people is the only way at present in which many craft skills are acquired. Experience in other countries has demonstrated that older workers with appropriate background experience can be given an adequate skill in many of these occupations through systematic courses far shorter than an apprenticeship. Where shortages of particular skills are apparent it does not seem sensible to restrict training to young people on apprenticeships.

6.22 We believe that it is important to consider ways of increasing the opportunities for those willing and able to learn craft skills. Shorter apprenticeships will help. So would moves to recognise pre-apprenticeship educational qualifications as entitling the holder to shorter apprenticeship periods. For example, currently students with vocational leaving certificates get no credit for their qualifications. Giving credit for relevant qualifications would attract beter-educated school-leavers into apprenticeship. Systematic off-the-job training will also attract more able entrants to craft occupations, as well as shorter apprenticeship times, especially if the whole of the first year after school could be spent in full-time vocational training. The team believes that careful consideration should be given to developing a comprehensive range of one-year full-time courses in establishments which have an industrial atmosphere (e.g. hours, discipline) and perhaps where the subjects taught have been agreed by both sides of industry. Such courses could be followed by on-the-job training for two or three years as necessary, backed up by short intensive training modules off the job.

TRAINING SERVICES FOR INDUSTRY

6.23 *General.* AnCO is already providing a number of services to individual industrial firms, partly on a repayment basis. We consider that there will be an increasing need for the central provision of services. For instance, AnCO should not only provide firms with training instructors, but also take instructors into training centres to receive tuition paid for by AnCO while salaries are still paid by the instructors' firms. Provision of training modules and kits with standard syllabuses should also be considered. Individual firms would not find it economic to provide such services for themselves. We recommend that AnCO should experiment freely with various services, not necessarily on a full repayment cost basis. This is likely in many cases to prove cheaper than the effort to provide the training directly through AnCO.

6.24 The Irish Management Institute is currently undertaking research in consultation with AnCO to assess future requirements for management training. We consider that the development of a comprehensive management training programme is necessary for Irish industry to prosper in the EEC. The IMI already offers a wide range of popular senior management courses on specialist techniques which attract support from most of the large Irish firms. We were favourably impressed with the availability of this type of management training, and urge that the IMI should continue its attempts to ensure that the structure and content is systematically related to current and future Irish management requirements. A greater attempt does need to be made to attract chief executives of organisations to advanced management courses, and we welcome the creation of a branch of the IMI to deal specifically with this problem. Two areas where the administration of management training might be improved are the selection and follow-up of trainees. A more active selection policy would guide training effort in the most profitable direction and follow-up will assist in the diffusion of improved management techniques throughout firms in which only a small number of executives are able to benefit from formal training.

6.25 An evaluation of the Irish Management-training effort can only be done against the background of the particular management problems of the Irish economy. It is possible to identify three quite different types of firm operating in Ireland – a relatively small but growing number of foreign-owned modern enterprises selling in fast-growing markets, a number of large, Irish-owned firms, primarily in the food, drink and textile industries, and a large number of small concerns engaged in small-scale agricultural, manufacturing and commercial activities. These different types of firm have very different management training requirements. The larger firms require fairly sophisticated training facilities in business skills such as finance, marketing, project control etc., designed to supplement technical or academic qualifications with the skills necessary to translate professional qualifications with the skills necessary to translate professional qualifications into effective business management. With a policy of active attraction to new foreign investment in operation, the provision of well-trained Irish managers is vital for both the successful establishment of incoming firms and their integration into the Irish business environment. It is important that IMI facilities for this type of training should meet the requirements of the new industry programme and should be specifically geared to that programme.

6.26 The large number of small firms also have a vital role to play in Irish economic progress, filling the gaps in the economy left by the larger enterprises and providing a source of new ideas and fresh enterprise. The need to maximise the contribution of the small firm sector is all the more pressing in a period of accelerating technical and economic change when Ireland is taking the first steps towards economic integration with the other EEC countries.

6.27 Specialist block release courses are well suited to the senior executive of a large modern enterprise, but not to the owner/manager of a small firm whose knowledge of management techniques is probably small and who is too deeply involved in the day to day business of his firm to spend several weeks away on an IMI course. The type of management training he requires is also different from the executive in the larger firm. His primary need is to build up a comprehensive but fairly basic level of accounting, marketing and labour management skills. We saw some evidence of management courses designed to meet what appears to be the very pressing needs of the owner/manager, but recommend a much greater concentration of effort on this particular problem.

6.28 The IMI is already operating a Programme for Smaller Business which has many of the attributes required of this type of specialised management training. Most of the courses are run for specific industrial sectors so that the subject matter can be related specifically to the task of managing a small firm in any given sector. Since the beginning of this programme in 1967, approximately 1,500 owner/managers of firms with under 100 employees have attended courses each year, and the IMI estimate that one-third of all owner/managers have attended at least one training course. This would still seem to be inadequate to meet the very real need for improved management in many small traditional Irish firms. We would like to see an expansion of the IMI programme to offer greater opportunities for owner/managers to receive periodic training in basic management techniques and particular problems of their own industries. We would also like to see an expansion in the current programme for in-company training and advice which is particularly well suited to the requirements of the small firm owner-manager.

SUPERVISORY TRAINING

6.29 There is a shortage of qualified supervisors and we recommend that AnCO should encourage the provision of supervisory training schemes in firms' training programmes. The team note that the IMI and the Institute of Supervisors have worked with AnCO to revise the syllabus for the relevant diploma and to produce student and teacher manuals; such co-operation should be continued. We recommend also that management training programmes should emphasize the importance of the recruitment of supervisors and of a proper understanding of their role.

HOTEL AND CATERING TRADES TRAINING

6.30 The Council for Education, Recruitment and Training for the Hotel Industry (CERT) has wide experience of the special problems of training for the hotel trade. However, the team does not feel that the problems of training in the hotel trade are so different as to justify the continuing independence of CERT from AnCO. We think it would be logical to extend AnCO's operations to cover not simply CERT's specialism of hotel training, but also restaurants and canteens.

AGRICULTURAL TRAINING

6.31 About one quarter of the labour force is employed in the agricultural sector and we were impressed with the range of training opportunities available. Given the importance of agriculture in the Irish economy it is not surprising to find that training in this sector is well established. We are certain that training in agriculture will continue to be important, particularly if the full benefits of EEC membership are to be gained, and we consider that it will be increasingly important for the training of people in agriculture to concentrate more than in the past on simple management training and on skills which might be helpful in the development of local processing of farm produce. Also, as technological knowledge increases, systems for spreading this information, such as are already provided by the Department of Agriculture and Fisheries and the Agricultural Advisory Service, will become increasingly important and their use should be encouraged at the training stage so that full benefit can be derived from the technological developments.

TRAINING FOR THE SERVICE INDUSTRIES

6.32 Provision for the service industries appears inadequate. Service industry has a major role to play in economic development and some thought might be given to the problem of determining training needs and providing Government assistance for the provision of training opportunities.

EDUCATION AND THE LABOUR MARKET

6.33 The basic function of the education process is to prepare individuals for their future role in society. Employment is a major feature of that role. Educational facilities should have regard to employment opportunities in the range and scale of courses they offer. The Department of Education has already made a major effort to improve the contribution of the education system to the preparation of individuals entering the labour market. They have expanded the provision of technical college education and are introducing community schools which have as a major objective the extension of facilities for the teaching of technical and work-related subjects. However, considerable problems remain.

6.34 Secondary education opportunities in Ireland vary from area to area. Much secondary education is academically-oriented with apparently little regard for labour market opportunities and requirements. A broad range of both academic and technical courses should be available to all secondary students and examinations might be standardised and offered in both academic and technical subjects and a mix of the two.

6.35 The Regional Technical Colleges have a primary role to play in the provision of trained manpower. They should be closely involved with local industrial and commercial training requirements and operational schemes, and seen as providing the systematic off-the-job element in training local skilled manpower. The current expansion programme is both necessary and welcome.

6.36 We formed the impression that the relationship between AnCO and the vocational education system is not effective. We think a closer relationship should be established and suggest the setting up of a joint committee to advise on content of syllabuses.

6.37 One special problem relevant to the expansion of the training effort in Ireland is that of emigration. Regardless of the way training is financed (except by a private self-financing loans scheme) an increased training programme might see much of the benefit lost to the Irish economy via emigration. Indeed as the level of training improves the work-force might become still more ready to move as Irish graduate training experience has suggested. A kind of international levy/grant system has interesting theoretical possibilities, and Ireland's participation in the European Social Fund and European Regional Fund might present the opportunity to work out some suitable arrangement. Lump sum transfers from countries benefiting from Irish training on an agreed bilateral basis might be another possibility for compensating for the outflow of trained labour from Ireland.

VII

MANPOWER POLICY IN IRELAND: A CONCLUDING INTERPRETATION

7.1 The choice of measures and the organisational framework of the manpower policy of a country is to a large extent determined and may thus be constrained by its historical traditions and the social and political situation. Discussion of national policies to be meaningful in an international forum must take account of all these considerations and constraints and concentrate on problems of a more general character, say where experience from one country may be of value for other countries. We have attempted to present and discuss Irish manpower policy in a general framework and point where Irish experience might be of value for other countries or where experience from other countries might be of value for the Irish. This is as far as an international examination team can go as it is impossible to make final judgements about which of another country's policies are good or bad.

7.2 As has been underlined in the preceding paragraphs the general character of manpower policy as a concept in economic analysis is far from clear. In any case there exist side by side two quite different approaches in the OECD countries:

(*a*) One approach stresses the problems in stabilisation policy of combining high employment with moderate inflationary pressures. Actual policies will then aim – within an active general demand management policy – to diminish structurally high unemployment with the minimum impact on inflation generating pressures and hopefully a decrease of inflationary pressures in the shortage sectors. This policy can be conducted in a number of ways: increasing demand selectively in the sectors with excess supply by direct expenditure or by subsidisation, decreasing expenditure or by selective taxation, or by attempting to increase mobility from slack to shortage sectors to alleviate imbalances.

(*b*) Another approach stresses the development and growth objectives and would attempt to create new jobs in areas with high unemployment and increase labour mobility from low productivity sectors to sectors with higher productivity. This approach tends to stress the necessity of speeding up a development process and overlooks the problems caused by transition between sectors in the growth process.

7.3 In practice it is difficult or may be meaningless to distinguish between the two different approaches and there will always be a growth aspect in the stabilisation-problem oriented policy and vice versa. Our study of the measures used in Irish manpower policy seems to indicate a stress on the development and growth approach.

7.4 This brings us back to the key question about the general character of Irish manpower policy. In the preceding chapters we have drawn attention to the fundamental imbalances in the Irish economy – high unemployment, trade deficit and considerable emigration. We have also observed that domestic inflation has continued at a relatively rapid rate while at the same time independent exchange rate policies have not been included in the range of economic policies. The continuing character of imbalances in the economy, when set against a background of somewhat limited macro-economic policies, suggests that the attempt to alleviate these imbalances by the use of manpower policies has set the policies a task for which they are fundamentally unsuitable. They appear to have been used as general subsidies to marginal employment across the whole economy, and may thus have been used to some extent as a substitute for more fundamental changes in macro-economic policy. This analysis may help to explain the apparent inability of an expanding manpower programme to deal with the problems of unemployment and inflation. The lack of success may not be due to the use of inefficient or unsuitable manpower policy measures, but an indication that the policies have not been wholly appropriate to the task they have been required to perform.

OECD SALES AGENTS
DEPOSITAIRES DES PUBLICATIONS DE L'OCDE

ARGENTINA – ARGENTINE
Carlos Hirsch S.R.L.,
Florida 165, BUENOS-AIRES.
☎ 33-1787-2391 Y 30-7122

AUSTRALIA – AUSTRALIE
B.C.N. Agencies Pty, Ltd.,
161 Sturt St., South MELBOURNE, Vic. 3205.
☎ 69.7601
658 Pittwater Road, BROOKVALE NSW 2100.
☎ 938 2267

AUSTRIA – AUTRICHE
Gerold and Co., Graben 31, WIEN 1.
☎ 52.22.35

BELGIUM – BELGIQUE
Librairie des Sciences
Coudenberg 76-78, B 1000 BRUXELLES 1.
☎ 13.37.36/12.05.60

BRAZIL – BRESIL
Mestre Jou S.A., Rua Guaipá 518,
Caixa Postal 24090, 05089 SAO PAULO 10.
☎ 256-2746/262-1609
Rua Senador Dantas 19 s/205-6, RIO DE JANEIRO GB. ☎ 232-07. 32

CANADA
Information Canada
171 Slater, OTTAWA. KIA 0S9.
☎ (613) 992-9738

DENMARK – DANEMARK
Munksgaards Boghandel
Nørregade 6, 1165 KØBENHAVN K.
☎ (01) 12 69 70

FINLAND – FINLANDE
Akateeminen Kirjakauppa
Keskuskatu 1, 00100 HELSINKI 10. ☎ 625.901

FRANCE
Bureau des Publications de l'OCDE
2 rue André-Pascal, 75775 PARIS CEDEX 16.
☎ 524.81.67
Principaux correspondants :
13602 AIX-EN-PROVENCE : Librairie de l'Université. ☎ 26.18.08
38000 GRENOBLE : B. Arthaud. ☎ 87.25.11
31000 TOULOUSE : Privat. ☎ 21.09.26

GERMANY – ALLEMAGNE
Verlag Weltarchiv G.m.b.H.
D 2000 HAMBURG 36, Neuer Jungfernstieg 21
☎ 040-35-62-501

GREECE – GRECE
Librairie Kauffmann, 28 rue du Stade,
ATHENES 132. ☎ 322.21.60

ICELAND – ISLANDE
Snaebjörn Jónsson and Co., h.f.,
Hafnarstræti 4 and 9, P.O.B. 1131,
REYKJAVIK. ☎ 13133/14281/11936

INDIA – INDE
Oxford Book and Stationery Co. :
NEW DELHI, Scindia House. ☎ 47388
CALCUTTA, 17 Park Street. ☎ 24083

IRELAND – IRLANDE
Eason and Son, 40 Lower O'Connell Street,
P.O.B. 42, DUBLIN 1. ☎ 01-41161

ISRAEL
Emanuel Brown :
35 Allenby Road, TEL AVIV. ☎ 51049/54082
also at :
9, Shlomzion Hamalka Street, JERUSALEM.
☎ 234807
48 Nahlath Benjamin Street, TEL AVIV.
☎ 53276

ITALY – ITALIE
Libreria Commissionaria Sansoni :
Via Lamarmora 45, 50121 FIRENZE. ☎ 579751
Via Bartolini 29, 20155 MILANO. ☎ 365083
Sous-dépositaires :
Editrice e Libreria Herder,
Piazza Montecitorio 120 00186 ROMA.
☎ 674628
Libreria Hoepli, Via Hoepli 5, 20121 MILANO.
☎ 865446
Libreria Lattes, Via Garibaldi 3, 10122 TORINO.
☎ 519274
La diffusione delle edizioni OCDE è inoltre assicurata dalle migliori librerie nelle città più importanti.

JAPAN – JAPON
OECD Publications Centre,
Akasaka Park Building,
2-3-4 Akasaka,
Minato-ku
TOKYO 107. ☎ 586-2016
Maruzen Company Ltd.,
6 Tori-Nichome Nihonbashi, TOKYO 103,
P.O.B. 5050, Tokyo International 100-31.
☎ 272-7211

LEBANON – LIBAN
Documenta Scientifica/Redico
Edison Building, Bliss Street,
P.O.Box 5641, BEIRUT. ☎ 354429 – 344425

THE NETHERLANDS – PAYS-BAS
W.P. Van Stockum
Buitenhof 36, DEN HAAG. ☎ 070-65.68.08

NEW ZEALAND – NOUVELLE-ZELANDE
The Publications Officer
Government Printing Office
Mulgrave Street (Private Bag)
WELLINGTON, ☎ 46.807
and Government Bookshops at
AUCKLAND (P.O.B. 5344). ☎ 32.919
CHRISTCHURCH (P.O.B. 1721). ☎ 50.331
HAMILTON (P.O.B. 857). ☎ 80.103
DUNEDIN (P.O.B. 1104). ☎ 78.294

NORWAY – NORVEGE
Johan Grundt Tanums Bokhandel,
Karl Johansgate 41/43, OSLO 1. ☎ 02-332980

PAKISTAN
Mirza Book Agency, 65 Shahrah Quaid-E-Azam,
LAHORE 3. ☎ 66839

PHILIPPINES
R.M. Garcia Publishing House,
903 Quezon Blvd. Ext., QUEZON CITY,
P.O. Box 1860 – MANILA. ☎ 99.98.47

PORTUGAL
Livraria Portugal,
Rua do Carmo 70-74. LISBOA 2. ☎ 360582/3

SPAIN – ESPAGNE
Libreria Mundi Prensa
Castelló 37, MADRID-1. ☎ 275.46.55
Libreria Bastinos
Pelayo, 52, BARCELONA 1. ☎ 222.06.00

SWEDEN – SUEDE
Fritzes Kungl. Hovbokhandel,
Fredsgatan 2, 11152 STOCKHOLM 16.
☎ 08/23 89 00

SWITZERLAND – SUISSE
Librairie Payot, 6 rue Grenus, 1211 GENEVE 11.
☎ 022-31.89.50

TAIWAN
Books and Scientific Supplies Services, Ltd.
P.O.B. 83, TAIPEI.

TURKEY – TURQUIE
Librairie Hachette,
469 Istiklal Caddesi,
Beyoglu, ISTANBUL, ☎ 44.94.70
et 14 E Ziya Gökalp Caddesi
ANKARA. ☎ 12.10.80

UNITED KINGDOM – ROYAUME-UNI
H.M. Stationery Office, P.O.B. 569, LONDON
SE1 9 NH, ☎ 01-928-6977, Ext. 410
or
49 High Holborn
LONDON WC1V 6HB (personal callers)
Branches at: EDINBURGH, BIRMINGHAM, BRISTOL, MANCHESTER, CARDIFF, BELFAST.

UNITED STATES OF AMERICA
OECD Publications Center, Suite 1207,
1750 Pennsylvania Ave, N.W.
WASHINGTON, D.C. 20006. ☎ (202)298-8755

VENEZUELA
Libreria del Este, Avda. F. Miranda 52,
Edificio Galipán, Aptdo. 60 337, CARACAS 106.
☎ 32 23 01/33 26 04/33 24 73

YUGOSLAVIA – YOUGOSLAVIE
Jugoslovenska Knjiga, Terazije 27, P.O.B. 36,
BEOGRAD. ☎ 621-992

Les commandes provenant de pays où l'OCDE n'a pas encore désigné de dépositaire peuvent être adressées à :
OCDE, Bureau des Publications, 2 rue André-Pascal, 75775 Paris CEDEX 16
Orders and inquiries from countries where sales agents have not yet been appointed may be sent to
OECD, Publications Office, 2 rue André-Pascal, 75775 Paris CEDEX 16

OECD PUBLICATIONS
2, rue André-Pascal, 75775 Paris Cedex 16

No. 33 531 - 1974
PRINTED IN FRANCE